Route 57
#13

This issue of *Route 57* is a lucky
thirteen, a treasure chest of text,
a vortex of so many fine words.
Writing is a scening of idea,
idea as language, crafted, shaped,
turned, conjured into being
by the imagination at work in the
world. And this issue brims
with ideas, stories, analyses of
experience, games among the
words. Dip into the treasure chest
and such things will rise to your
consciousness as true gifts
from book to you. Inside you'll
encounter, variously and as if
in passing: the gold and sloe eyes
of the heron, tattoos on the skin
of a mammoth building, crushed
rocks and unwritten books,
the Valleys scarped and shaped,
criss-crossing beelines, airborne
anatomies, a susurrus through
nothing, the unexpected tangle of
markets, glass-eyed mechanics,

the distant empty blue of the sky, the roaring noise-lessness of gales, stream of bloody blossom leaves, calligraphy of brick and mortar, witches clad in mud brown gowns, cackling suns, white lines of engine noise, pale and lobstered skin, carboniferous grit, a cat called William Carlos Williams, the smell of pure language, fear rippling floorboards, decaying toes, monkey-bars of DNA, the darkness of closed eyelid, buttery kisses, forgetful dreaming bodies, a bag of bags and pegs, yawning coats, the crackle of corn, the hive mind of a comprehensive school, swamps, snow, ash, fire, overlapping neon, Promethean flame, strange pumpkin looking things, giggly blur and twilight, cannulae clogged and powdered with plaster, apathetic cars, cavalcades

of shadows and difficult water,
waves of thudding ink, velvet veins,
the edge of reason, gizzard-face
dogs, elongated shh sounds, resonance of location, breaking world
and shaking faith, caterpillars
on cheetahs, the chink of teeth
on glass, Hondas of paradise
blue, man-made clouds, inevitable
taboo, silver buttons glinting
in moonlight, sky-lit houses of
white with lab-like greenhouses,
a plunge of straight black rock,
bland porridge-like walls, intimate
liaisons with the KGB, blank,
white flesh, snapping bones and
popping cartilage, suspended
teacups, the chatter of crowds and
chill of the air, the mystification
of meat, wild mountains and peaceful prairies, food deserts, a collective mass of identical twins, a
radical theory collective. And that's
not all: the book is a collective too,

Editors

Ágnes Lehóczky
Ben Allen
Grace Cohen
Veronica Fibisan
Aidan Jenner
Samuel Kendall
Amy Kinsman
Alex Marsh
Katie Smart

Foxgloves

I

It could have been *foie gras,* no less, something smooth
slithers between lips, though muffled in a mouthful
a second time, scattered in the chime of champagne floats
colliding across table tops, then, eventual gurgling.

Silver penny bubbles trail across the tongues
that work away an afternoon, worming bitter tales
over sour dough, mouths the *ah*-s and *oh*-s
to the tune of brunch-time etiquette, here in the bleached

indent into city life where English tea houses relish
rare sunlight and parade their store fronts with European
coffee-shop tables, fill the reverent brunchers, now
engrossed in poppy-seed bagels and cucumber water—

who exercise taste buds honed to the delectable,
to the aromatic rising off of fine china
                    lemon zest
                    then,
the stink of vermin.
Foul, sweating out their pelt under October sunshine.

Behold the inner-city nomad:
as a shadow creeping as slowly as the sun rises,
as a bug on a distant surface where the
high street is drab, dull and melancholy,
stick-like six legs scuttle over monochrome—
                    alien
here, in the groves where paving stones are broken into green space,
flowers, new trees, fallow in grey fields,
where young blood congregate and empathise with the ever-thinning ozone,
                    sewing kit in hand
                    soy beans and plasters
                    a thin string of humility
                    ready for threading.

Empathise, still, as the vagrant lingers—paws outstretched, inching over table tops,
        unmistakably *here*
dead-eyed and high boasting a dark concave, pale skin and pink sores, the seeds of
rough sleeping. Sulphite-liver-stuffing from the over counter brownbag-cider
        numbs loneliness.
Threatens the end of benedict, yolk bleeds down into the loaf.

Bare pearly white tegs, the *I'm sorry* eyes—
change buried in the nooks of jean pockets, too many turns of a limp wrist,
that, that that is,
that is,

utters nothing, more than
red cheek stuttering.
Bills are split, waiters tipped, out tipping the other.

II

It should have ended in the wheel arches.
Where loose bolts are free to break bones
and sheer momentum forms stock cubes.
To pull oily clumps from the tread of old tires
—is not cruel—
when nerves are blown like a misused fuse box
thought and no feeling
mind wandering with the romantics.

Shore waters roar against quay walls,
sends black and white war birds bumbling in the tumult.
I crouch, waiting for wings to hit
more-bat-like in this darkness, street lights reach out
small hands, smaller fingers, thin whispers on a black landscape
of winged-things sure to sing to my in-an-hour blues.
Taxi cab climbs the concourse—careers towards, through, across,
leaves a sad mass writhing in existence.

Sings a swan song,
one soprano scream
or squeal,
dissonant to those sea birds that prevail
        somewhere
above me,   hawks at the diner
now,
more vulture—expressing distinct carnivore.

The victim slithers as I shiver,
cold caught in the wind coming off of the sea front,
drags broken bones and two lost limbs
two more testing out an axis across the gravel.

To be, man distilled.
            Incarnate as a Father who stands with a boulder
            towering over limp chickens, to break the backs of rats,
        to be, the brutalist
            and build pillars through the firmament,
            concrete walls keep out tender feelings,
            scatter this stranger
            creeping in the stairwells
            asleep in the wheel arches—
            to send bad thoughts flying, scarring.

Except this is no stranger,

they morph with every second into something more familiar. Awakens feeling
buried deep in a foreign vault, lost in some strange alcove. Teeth, lips, nose.
Stretching   as some snout. Takes me home, to the single bed in a box room
where Mother reads from a Dahl book and makes this mass coy, sly, inputs definite
intelligentsia   vulpes-vulpes   then, an adaption given in adolescence

when lifeless becomes life   though the cruel nature of it all brings me to
Ted's thinking,

                    one hot stink. The limp and the blood clot.

More, peeling back dusty covers of a thought book even I did not know I owned, a
recollection races to my frontal lobe, I see your ears and eyes, the inch thick
hairline dressing down your bones,   in you, I see my trusted mutt. I see a
kindness, I see four legs trotting in green fields and a bundle of

          Good girls.

Reject the brutalist, let me strike a chord and resolve this in some common song,
the cold table of a veterinarian awaits, remain alive till we see those surgery lights—

                    though,
                    I see in my own conjectures
                    that when thoughts were free and nimble in
                    romantic recollection
                    to wander with Wordsworth through an alpine pass—
          you have crawled,
          two legs broken like bicycle spokes,
          flown in every angle,
          a spine tangled into twenty knots,
          through the darkness and away from me.

All that remains are the small shards you thought hapless and a bloody puddle
collecting on the concrete. In it I see hesitation and hear our song, unresolved.

III

The pieces are there.
              Jigsaw puzzled as the first napkin stumbles across the parkway, darts
along the estuary weaving between the feet and legs of coffee shop connoisseurs
and outdoor table sets, hand tarnished, worn down to a primer. It flies unobserved,
hiding signs of bleeding in the two corners creased up and overturned in its
approach. Stops for a second too long a few feet from my own pair, though far
enough from the high street and the stone faces tucking into croissants and
distilled fruit teas. Presents a blood spot.

Light, as a paper cut as a pink-thing
raw and red lily blisters
a falling stream of poppy seeds
flowers in the ridges of dead skin.

Mistaken for caring, I shake my head. All of this, two stains an inch from the other,
being ketchup or cranberry—anything and all before the blood of another, black
and vulgar as a shadow cast by the chic street's delectable. A second limps and
shows four to eyes that wander on the liver speckled drifter; kinder souls part with
copper and stray silvers mistakenly taken from cotton pockets: sends the space
invader back into the breeze.

A stream of bloody blossom leaves
the heels of two worn workmen's boots
cotton balls off of fingerless foxgloves
boasting pale white rigid finger-things.

My neck bows as a black mass invades peripheries, third and fourth come crawling,
unmistakably—here—soaked in a deep shade. They shuffle at my feet, lend red ply
to shoelaces. Now, billowing in the wind, a thousand marked napkins take me,
rising as a cruel swan on the river bank. Parades tainted plumage, stretches
blistered wings and a new bill—blue from rough sleeping.

Bone eyed and clawless,
new scabs and callus,,
fingernails too long caught
scratching against the earth

paddle in the bloodstreams
stray legs and polyethylene,
comes a body from it all
strange, lucid, dirty
gutter scrubber

though,

with eyes familiar
to our own
as the fox to dogs
in them see a ghost
legs in spokes
shades of hesitation
and
ridged lifelessness, less I move
to be, the Samaritan
here, in this red single-ply cyclone.

Ben Allen

Storm on Norbreck Prom

The spray cutting our faces
the only thing that reminds us
that the sea is trying to break out
of the darkness below
shaking the bars   screaming
we taunt it
with the wind at our backs   forcing us into confidence
forcing us closer to the edge
away from the old band stand   too stubborn
to give up and slip away from the storm
too bored
to give up standing so close   to death
too naïve at seventeen   to picture
mortality slipping   too focused on
the roaring noiselessness of the gale
to hear the sound of barking
and an old man crying out

Chad Bentley

Still

Yellow, an inoffensive choice
something to do with sun
or spring. Suitable for either,
suitable for both. You once said
you wouldn't mind twins, still
there were only really two choices
and we didn't mind, not really.
Just happy waiting to be happy.
Not knowing left too much open
other people said, we said it was
exciting, delaying things until
he / she was here. Even if there were
complications we would still   it didn't bare thinking about
it was a worst case   the worst case
without a   you just don't expect it these days
we'd never even considered it because
surely the easiest thing a baby can do is
just be born.

Chad Bentley

Two minutes

In the silence of those mornings I could
picture the last leaves fall from the beech above,
hear them collect in drifts behind the graves.

As if the cars had stopped on the tarmac
with hazards on and windows wound down,
to let in the still, as if they had at least tried.

Perhaps even the aircraft were grounded,
as I recall not one blemish on the
width of azure stretched taut above our heads.

Only the church spire and parapet
—steeped in light that made us all tall—were
allowed to interrupt the distant empty blue.

I see the empty faces of the parade
staring at the blank spot beyond their noses;
in Sunday best and winter coats, fresh pressed

navy three-piece suits with last year's dry-clean
receipt screwed up inside and a pocket full
of hymn sheets from all the years before.

A semblance of grief from embroidered saints;
on Whit-walk standards held high by the choir,
a keening November wind filled them like sails.

Simon Broomhead

The tunnel

I dreamt I was driving with a child in the passenger's seat and as we approached the tunnel its black and yellow pendulum was industrial trellis and could drop at any moment like a hammer. The child ducked and held his breath upon entering, superstitious, feeling blinkered, like the cone-headed dog just home from the vet, unable to nab at the itch in his folds and creases. I urged him to focus on counting the hingeless doors that pop up, or the loose-hanging wire above, and not the fact we were now at a conspicuous distance from the princess being chauffeured in front. Tunnels you can see out of, like the Pont de l'Alma in Paris, can't be entrusted with secrets, and did you know the mind of a child can dissemble, is still to lay its bridge supports to push against, or bore into, and what adult knows from where we're likely to emerge anyway? This child wanted to ask about the men who drive wanting photographs, who will make new incidents just for the event of a good photograph, and others who seek gratefulness, a kind of gratitude for their own elevation. Shadows of pillars flick by. Now he wants me to tell again the story of the glass-eyed mechanic, whose right eye was snatched through the side window of his Mercedes by the hand of a motorcyclist flung after an errant piece of cable-tie, or loose-hanging wire, likely got stuck in his bike's engine or wheel. Incidents flick by, quicker than their events. Did the motorcyclist need gratefulness, a kind of gratitude for his elevation? And what if our rear-view mirror is a liar, and the scene behind the car is collapsing, like a plastic bottle singed with a clipper lighter? Or the tunnel doesn't keep its side of the bargain. But see if you can keep holding, I said to the child, the lit ceiling is, for now, still turning

Sam Buchan-Watts

Moving

There's something in the air
says maybe tomorrow it'll snow.

I'm walking back to a new house
from somebody else's bus stop.

A shopping bag's caught in a tree.
A moon glows in a neighbour's window.

The key works, though I could be anyone,
and the front room's an unfinished jigsaw

of boxes. The streetlights warm up
as the kettle boils, and I picture

my old place, its cupboards all open,
its rooms filling slowly with snow.

Joe Caldwell

The best part of the afternoon

Not the museums or churches,
the square of statues clinging to their
thin coats of watery sunlight. Instead,

the unexpected tangle of markets:
shacks offering brandy and pretzels,
meats frying in alien spices,

musicians gleaming in the park beyond
the last stall. Beyond them, ice skaters
riding the dusk, tracing fleeting tracks
on a field holding its mirror to the sky.

Joe Caldwell

3,943

The alphabet sung the distance,
key-tapped radiowaves
        that the submarines poured into their
metal shells and bulleted back across the surface.

A chair creaked softly. Black hair was push pulled by white fingers,
clawed into a lump
and corn danced in fields I've never tasted, the thick heads
buffeting into one another, breaking
to the sound of feet.
The breeze called again, and again.
There was some thing, some cloud, some bird flying south …

        She kisses her slick bubble-gum teeth white, whiter
        than wet chalk to stone,
        snapping each pop back to jaw,
        I hate her for it.

        I hate that invisible face with a sadness I cannot name.
        The boys wait, off stage.
        I will hate them too.

The crack of a glass beaker
and the hiss of fingernails
ghosting over skin.

      The radiowaves are silent. Nothing grows anymore.

So a susurrus through nothing,
no trees, no nests of cotton,
this alien skin, alien face
age pulling at it like a surgeon's knife—
In this alien bed
my flesh starts to doubt, now I'm not so sure…
Dirt under fingernails

      No, that was another.

Now how many endings stand against my teeth?
Soft skin and cold pink bathwater, bath
pulling from the mastic.

Here with a bright spectral face glowing in the evening,
the caught breath of the conflicted
      the best or the worst

Either way it's done.
The black crawls to the floor.
For better or worse.

Grace Cohen

Chrysalis

Burn
my new tongue
on this old whisper,
a cold burn, continually
cut me, into loving this—salt
and peppering scalp with knotted
fingers, over and over again, so let me
eat this, watch it, there is no solid, no one
voice only me and I, the continual delusion
of wholesomeness, be my vigilante, stalking
synapses for error, I am the ninth edition, I am
the first, editing and re-editing, breaking open,
introducing the tenth, this situation is not conducive
to writing so pour me another, pour me ten more, no,
peppermint, the smell of a locker room, a wet room, pad
pad my feet, flicker, stop. This smells like something sweeter,
the aftermath, an anthology of selves, document the many arms,
devour all with a lens, slowly forgetting myself, break in, this is the
politics of meat, me in the middle, outraged and tremble, hiding them
with shaky hands, throw it down now, suck out the marrow, this isn't it,
I am sure, but what is after the aftermath, maybe the ice caps are lonely,
they are and I can hear them and the walls are pouring into my shot glass, a
symphony, wow, only one smaller, who is the next, keep cutting the fat,
judging weight, vacuum pack, line me up, who is this—an involuntary
twitching of the leg, maximum confusion, terror, terror, the bulb
has blown, crush it down to synthesise, rip up the carpet,
rip up them all, huddled over the bathtub, docile bodies,
the crackle of expansion, pull it back, puberty
drew my skin into constellations, star maps
to see me through, now the charts
are but traces, now the
lines are dead.

Grace Cohen

bellum se ipsum alet

There was too much to eat that night,
(too many bodies) my mouth
cut a thousand mirrors,
picking bones from our teeth,
it was a wonder
      how in the glut of it all
nobody choked.

A slide of skins, a swarming tide
of vacant eyes
      and scales.
Bodies collecting at feet, the rotting
bounty, the mad preacher,
dynamite fishing in silver rivers,
calling God down
upon the stinking offspring.
Poison would not smell sweeter—

A hundred eyes
      anthraxing me
from a distance // no distance too wide
for airborne anatomies
behind it all, the men,
cold and quiet with now unnumbered eyes
a unnumbered bodies waiting,
so patiently,
for the first of us
to bite,

Grace Cohen

Nighthoney

Our beelines keep criss-crossing, how
And why don't these lights ever
Keep still
There comes the little bear
And there the great
Across the hill
Out of the woods
The predatory stars are falling
Descending on our
Sweet dreams

Mara-Daria Cojocaru

Rumination

God, my sheep and goats are yours

In the grass, yet
A number, red
A bluish speck
Paint in my pelt
But something greens
I chew upon
I stomach that
My God

Mara-Daria Cojocaru

Hiraeth

Behind the dam that holds back the floods,
There hides a place that's homesick for itself;
Polluting the fresh air, the town churns out a nausea
That funnels down the streets, by rows of houses, into cars
Stopped, winded, by the side of winding roads.
A sense of crisis precipitated only by the overhanging
Weight of the reservoir, is kept in check by but the rain's sermon.

In common with revolution, or a resolution
Of New Year's, many regret the settlement,
Now forever into the Valleys scarped and shaped,
For the sake of black gold. In their Rhondda-rhetoric
One hears talk of digging deep, of recovering
A past that did not exist, or at least from a terminal lack
Of care necessary, as befits an end-of-the-line drop-off point.

In pubs where bitter's served warm on tap,
A certain class of men will vent a nostalgia
Quite understated yet here stamped firm, as if a mark
Of high quality. What makes their eyes still further crack—
Or is that become steeled to the future?
The same process that left them milling about, that mixed
The hardness of souls with flexible labour laws, that militarised heritage.

To tour around the local cwms and tors
Is welcoming that wistfulness which fogs
The fells in clichés of Wales, either on foot
Or with woolly prose set to task sloganising turf.
Thus is Hiraeth strewn vaguely over hills,
Belying as they must the nature of life, what poverty exists
Under the auspices of farms and hearths, what essence extracted.

Not that a name means a thing, for where
Resides such elusive heartache also works hope.
The hinterland has always kept paradise its secret,
Though now inundated with opiates, amphetamines, and ket—
Stalks the land no spectre but a wraith.
It's Time! call tenant-landlords from overlooked vantage points,
And all go home, the morning to construct new mechanisms for coping.

Frederick Coombes

Live-birth

The old Gods still move. They step with earth-warm toes.
You remain lost in their memory—
unseen—unspoken
—equal and free.

I

They mingle with a half-remembered childhood   and draw
                              swift lines through cold assembly halls.
They beguile   flickering light bulbs and eke out the last
                              drops of candle wax.   Hot
          breathless promises above
                              stolen stories catch the eye and blink
     away in a moment.
Their bodies remain in unwritten words; naked characters without the spill
                              of blood or ink.
They are the movement of things:
the   shift   of   echoed   breath
     scattered   across   streets   stained with battle
          cries   rattling   in engines.
     This is the line that killed them.

II

                              Clouds that promised the end
                    have borne children already
                              too old to be sacrificed. You
                    stand unremarkable: lilting lips thick with an
                    unbranded bathroom cleaning product
Skin pocked   with kisses and bites
     flinches   at its the echo
               of a dry hand on their picked-bone pew,
                              too polite to sing or pray.
Known to all and expected
     like rain; your skull
                    scattered   on the pavement
with horror and rendition.

III

Palm like a blighted field, outstretched
               fingers twitch with a question, answered
with hard teeth; a prayer, canine shaped,
     calls for cleaner hospitals, calls for whiter walls, calls for warmer summers,
     better shower lotion,

double glazed duvet
wardrobe assembly instructions
revenge-porn light switch
that new carpet smell
a doggerland-dance
£4 wine
clogged nose
softly breathing in a quiet office
the feeling of Sunday on the skin
celery veins
a stranger's smile
grab her by the—
and the answer rings in cool ears.

Paper clings to your face, soiled with half-done sums.
The clock flicks its tongue in time to your pulse.

IV

You rest, buried in a nest that never starts and never
stops. The endless sweeping plane
bound with glossed pulp,
still clings to the mouth's red corners.
Lyrics catch
in the throat as dumb lumps.
Fat eggs that elude life like stones
slipping across ice.
A warm body
nourishes cold
lines curled into themselves;
Eyelids flicker against the sun.
A fat egg slips down the throat.

V

You became lost in crushed rock and unwritten books, to return
every month with vague ideas of what might be good. I checked the
pan had boiled with my hand thrust into it: an unlocked rage
through clenched jaws. Eyes like keys, polished but old and pushing
just wide of the mark.

A limp map unravels into a page of human schematics. Vague lines dilate
through blurred lips.
I stand
an empty vessel
and slip beneath
the ocean of you.

John Darley

Park Hill valentine

What I could not say I spelled out
in runes on a tomb; I tattooed
the skin of a mammoth building—
I LOVE YOU, see? Let me leave no doubt.

This city made us hard as nails,
sharp as knives; you cast down your eyes,
refused to look up at my love
as it towered above us, it failed.

WILL U MARRY ME? I left it
suspended, unanswered, unending
on the walkway, just in case,
where you gave me my head for heights.

Then one day the tomb raiders came,
saw an open invitation
and they retraced it in neon.
Beside this, your name slowly fades.

Kristina Diprose

Jamón Ibérico de Bellota

'A peasant becomes fond of his pig and is glad to salt away its pork.'
John Berger, *Why look at animals?*

Clamped to a bespoke stand, a slender leg
gold-skinned, fat-marbled, Velázquez red.

Black-hooved hogs flickered
on fire-lit walls of ancient caves,
still forage fragrant herbs
among holm oaks on the *dehesa*.

Through the *montanera*
snuffle-grunt among grasses for acorns
which give the flesh its nut-sweet flavour.

Winter is the time of sacrifice:
pack meat in salt, stir hot blood for *morcillo*,
wash guts in vinegar and lemon.

A pig is chosen, hefted onto a table-altar.
Men soothe and stroke the prone creature,
fear taints ungiven gifts.

Jenny Donnison

To be a heron

hone the art of stillness,
balance on limb-stem in green shallows,

at the margins of minnowed rivers,
silvered estuaries, stickleback streams.

Stand in timeless pose on stone
or on whalebone struts of abandoned boats,

a ghost the colour of cut flint
clouded in sun-sparked *Ephemera*.

Shade-cloak water with outspread wings.
Reprise primeval origins in kink-necked flight.

Stir silt with splayed feet
panning for invertebrate glints.

Focus gold and sloe eyes
on dart and glide in trailing weed

and having by heart the laws of refraction,
pierce surface deception with sabre beak.

Jenny Donnison

Cityscript

Try to hold the city's gaze,
but blink.
Breathe exhaust fumes,
tarmac, unrequited kinship.
Rehearse the words it wants to hear,
its script a calligraphy of brick and mortar.
Lines like roadworks,
concrete birthing concrete,
grit on the tongue.
It listens, impatient,
sighs streets unfurling.
They will find your edges, pull them apart,
close as the river, distant as the moon,
and in that distance, stirring the air,
sound on sleepless repeat: a circadian rhythm
played on paving slabs and glass,
never settling in the ear,
but in the memory of home,
your wayward yesterdays,
a crack in the tiles.

Peter S Dorey

South of site

Cleethorpes Beach, summer 2016

estuarine rivulets
a haunt of
[submerged hazards]
                              a
                              mazes
          a
          masses
signage directs   distorts maps

thicket thistle tops
tamper with the weather
witches clad in mud brown gowns

                                        rooftops settle
                                        sunk behind dune
                                        slightly above sea level
pedestrian access for birds
past fitties
                    to beach or strand
gull beaks fish pincers in pairs
                    from the shallows
at low tide
evidence exposed
sea dunes marshes   shift
                                        shortened days
darkened dampened drawn
                                        curtains of our chalet windows
                         inside
          our humanity settles
elegant bird tucks its wings
          a turnstone wintering

Veronica Fibisan

The traffic lights

Street corners, shadowed by spray painted brickwork that refuses to lend light. Standing above the terraces, piercing the clouds, I face it all. All the while displaying your ever-changing heart in wounds my body recently discovered.

Our eyes seldom meet in the faint moonlight. Yours are cotton wool balls, mine red. Road rage driving you further away from the delayed destination.

You hope for a green light, wanting to be certain that your speed will not be reckless. I see you sitting there through a constant amber gaze, counting digits under leather gloves.

Jack Field

The shampoo bottle

Shampoo. *The strength restorer.* Wash and rinse, you'll have stronger hair in just one week.

In that time, circles could be sat on, accidentally. Balls of stress repressed, then torn to lose their function. And the song you sung, or the hula-hooping in that autumn garden that you watched, years ago, with confusion and amazement all at once... It is all forgotten.

You could fast for seven days and lay in unchanged sheets, only moving for the shower's promises.

Jack Field

The cloud

Was it Orwell who described the Parisian sky as a cobalt wall?

We sit lifeless tonight, under a sun nearly set that cackles at each lowered beam. The world shaking with every stolen ray. But I see others walking in step with the carnival's rhythm, bragging with their ignorant limbs that the quake only affects me.

You ask me to answer, but I cannot, and so instead you tell me the words I speak inside my own mind. Harmonising your soft and gentle tones with my hard bass. You tell me in my words how, like great literature and music of centuries gone by, time cannot depreciate the chains of silk that we tie between ourselves and those who stroke our hearts.

Jack Field

Night walk by the River Don

Saturday. The city's out there dancing
and I'm suffused in alcoholic fug
sleeping in my clothes and dreaming some
night walk by the River Don where
Neepsend Lane plays tributary to
Penistone Road, where hostelry ghosts
of the Farfield Inn drink on, nine years
since the Don called an imperious last
orders, its waters rising as high as the bar
and here my feet make off northwest:
a lane flanked dense with thickets,
the freakish Don below, a carriageway
of bustling currents. I commute upriver,
the work of the dream awaiting and white
points of light, white lines of engine noise
reaching from the road beyond. A moment
comes when rumination's apt, when to
offer down my soles to stroke the surface
seems the fittest course. I mull, send texts
(the Don could take me if it wanted to),
and I can't vouch for unseen trees
falling in the forest, but my dream-state
absence here attests the Don still flows
when nobody is there. Its spate persists,
relentless, unabashed. Taking a cue, I
rise again and shun the lane to hold
fast to the bank, backtracking, soft-
stepping, taking two small falls to founder
in soft ground, still clambering implausible
ledges that narrow near to nought,
aware that if this mud dispels all friction,

balance elude us and my footing fail, I'll
dream a fatal dash against a concrete edge,
wake bewildered, wondering and unscathed.
Further up our way broadens and emerges
onto some industrial estate: undisturbed,
I dodge a barrier watched by rows of
empty windows, which disclose only
blankness, and an assumed panopticon of
CCTV lenses up in the gods. A shopfitter,
a tool parts supplier. I can't tell whether
they're going concerns or gone; we take
dereliction as read, scoping the city
that never wakes up. In the end I'm
circling one small section of some dirt track
shot with potholes, Hillsborough's lights
glaring over from across the way, playing
on the tarry, sluggish surface of the Don
to set a monochrome mosaic. The city
too, it seems, continues to exist alone
when I dream I'm somewhere else.
The only thing to do's retrace my steps.
Somewhere a security guard chuckles
as I cross his screen again. Back at the start,
just before the dream fades, there I am
baffled by a dumped bathtub I'd not
registered before, matter-of-fact
as elephants in rooms. I wake to find
my coat and boots bedaubed in river mud;
on my phone, each step recorded by
an app that tracks your way by GPS, and the
bathtub photographed, stark as a full stop.

Pete Green

The astronomer's wife

Her jealousies too absurd,
wordlessly livid, she
knits her knuckles, stares

over at the empty seat,
out to the shameless stars,
jangles her hair

across each solo hour,
blank as interstellar space,
straining her ears,

and summons the power
to size up her foe. How can it just
go on forever?

The plink of ice in gin
and edgy patter of her
calls to friends—

at least the return
of a comet can be
predicted with accuracy.

Of all the universe's
potential infidelities,
she endures the cruellest,

a rival too intangible to fight.
In the void
she can confront only,

lacking warmth or gravity,
the unimaginable, dark
distance between bodies.

Pete Green

Nada más

Beer crate seat on terraced terrain,
she sits in the valley of production.
Carried by her Spanish friend
to a place few like her could go.

'Hombre' Hombre, Hombre' echoes
 surround her, above, below, to the side
the campesinos greet and rally
against the dust, the heat, the exhaustion.

Avocados at her knees, she picks the crop.
Her Spanish friend picks oranges, lemons,
custard apples, salad onions around her.
They chatter in both tongues laughing.

An unforgiving sun ripens her skin,
He massages her back thoroughly,
her pale and lobstered skin covered in relief,
he nuzzles her neck, on the campo stage.

Avocados broken open by hungry hands
they eat and taste uncomplicated goodness,
sharing and feeding each other;
basking in the wholeness of their lives.

Produce ready for co-operative weighing
Her Spanish friend carries her to the lorry,
wheelchair slumped in the back, with
fruit, vegetables and olive tree netting.

Rich local wine seeps into their veins,
pan, queso, ensalada on their plates
as the onerous evening sun persists.
'Más?' he asks, 'Nada más, gracias' she smiles.

Ali Hayward

A granular particle

Grit had its way,
fouled my appliance—

as surely as a pea
stole sleep from a royal girl
or an errant nail saw a kingdom
lost or a swallowed fly,
the coroner said,
caused an elderly woman's death.

Grit halted my hoover,
so recently bought—

hefted below to the cellar
where plasterboard walls almost
meet floor, my Dirt Devil vac
choked on the city's foundational grit

that bore up the Reverend C.J. Street
penning sermons here in my home,
the 1911 census reports, ousted now
by my keyboard and mouse.

Carboniferous grit,
layered in a river's expanding bed,
buried by limestone, coal, mud,
trodden by dinosaurs, quarried
from sandstone scarps, up to the task
of shredding toughened grain,

grit eroding downstream,
finding its way.

Jenny Hockey

What went well

I lied to my Year Sevens. Fabricated the starter,
told them that adorning my refrigerator
was a note pawed in ink. I told them
it was written by William Carlos Williams,

my cat. The note had an apology for the fact
that the sweet plums were eaten by the cat.
He also opined that he was 'very bothered'
that his greed had been uncovered.

I worry now for the sanity of the students
as they ponder the 'is he, isn't he' existing creation.

Although there were no none animals 'not injured'

going forward I feel the need for prudence
and rechristen the cat for the next generation
in the tick box marked clearly for Schrödinger.

Gary Hughes

Thoughts on a waterway

I

From the hill, under the windmill,
the canal writes itself
for twenty eight miles
over flatlands, still-moving.

> In the mid-distance the sea speaks,
> and sometimes fails
> to say anything at all.

Reeds bend backwards idly,
while we ramble through
a tedious conversation,
along the waterway.
You say that I'm a liar.
I have found them though,
seen them for myself
in the yellow afternoon
that comes, warm, from my mouth.

Shall we chase words under the verges
into the clear unclear water?
You have told me often enough
that you'd like to go to the bottom.
I can't say I know entirely
what has been left there
but it has been due a dredging
for some years now.
Let's go, waist deep in.

> And when we get back,
> cold, sodden and solemn,
> with the smell of pure language
> burned into our noses
> we can sleep then, again.

II

> Barefoot on the grass,
> a sentence stands
> apologetically poised
> on your tongue's tip.

One rub of an eyelid eases out
a sound that falls saltily
over the crest of a cheek
and onto my coffeed lips
where silence finds an end.

On the out folded table inside,
that is covered by leaves
that we picked
        and scattered around
because we like letting spring in,
there is a mug of tea,
for us to drink over a book.
The rings stain brown
the milky pages, see.

The rings stained brown
the milky pages, see,
and the book,
ruined brilliantly in the reading,
is there to bend backwards
on the tube home
in the queasy air.
Dredge it for all its worth.

III

Tall girl, handsome girl.
I'll unmake you in a word girl,
while climbing the martello
that exposes itself
engraved on the horizon,
with my right eye.

On its top it is possible
to see thousands of caravans
that sit like scattered molars
as a radius for the town of Rye.
Pluck one and look under the pillow
for a word in the morning.

They have the look of still things
but can be moved
under certain conditions
which only people
who move caravans
and understand their heft know.
We all, at some point,
will be in that business.

And in carrying a tonne
of white blocks
down a man made river
it is quite probable
that those made girls
will come occasionally
to offer you a hand
in the chaos of the sentence
with words spilling into
the next unwritten field;
Shall I unmake them too?

IV

On the bridge that crosses
away from distraction,
bank to bank, over the canal,
away from distraction,
the yellow taste returns.
It twitches on the water
after sticks filled with lead
hit the surface and make outward ripples
that reach the edges and turn back
inward rippling to the very start,
almost into the margins.

We used to do that as children,
I don't know why,
didn't have to know why.
Instead we ran quick
to the other railing
to see which small piece
of wood would prevail
in our childish games,
didn't stick around
to think about non-existence,
or even watch the ripples.

V

You lost me down stream,
on solid-unsolid terrain,
shingles instead of grass,

shingles as opposed to grass,
        making efforts at finding
                a route to safety.

                It is more difficult, though,
        when the ground beneath foot
                gives way every seven steps,
and I tend to find that danger
                will take me home.

Retracing your steps,
        you see that everything
is malleable at our toes' tips.
                The grounds soft face does want to
                                take us back to the water.

At its bank, the canal lays itself, again,
        beneath our senses, still moving
long after purpose is discarded;
everything is malleable.

                        VI

                The sea speaks;
                sends us wind
                that whistles beneath
                autumn coloured iron
                into mind or sight
                to inflate flocks of words
                with gusts of noise.

                        Our home made,
                        in the easy silence.
                        by writing hands,
                        appears as a small black hut
                        complete with a red top.
                        It contains and releases,
                        every other day or so,
                        the work of mouths
                        down the channel.

                        VII

                        The Kingfisher darts
                        on blue feathered wings
                        as a half sight between
                        exchanged words.

She lowers to pluck
from the water,
with real precision
things not as they are
but as they could be,
and holds them fluttering
behind those reeds.

In the quiet hide,
on the canals side,
you watch for days
at the out folded table
to catch in suspense,
the thief of things,
wings feathered.

With just a glimpse,
the Kingfisher is lost
again between words
we've caught and understood,
and put away in untidy beds.

VIII

Frost announces itself
on windows in January;
a signature in blue,
that looks with worry
over the canal.

Its thick water struggles
to give us anything
but yellow Sundays
in the back of our eyes
gestured in by sleep.

Eighty five coffee spoons
in the porcelain sink wait
for the pipes to thaw.

The table set for writing
is piled with brown leaves
because we forgot
to take winter out.

Aidan Jenner

That night you saw the fox by the cot

See his hands—these claws learn the earth's shape,
Just as the bowstring in his mind sends him leaping
Away from the jaws of dogs. Their breath bubbles

In his bones now. You're forced
To watch him grow sleek and wise, reared on animal milk.
That night you saw the fox by the cot,

You missed the gentleness of its teeth round your baby's neck.
The long face questioned you then. You stared back,
Peeling layers of fear that had mildewed deep
Within the cupboards and windowpanes,

Fear that had rippled the floorboards, risen the yeast,
Entered the house through keyholes and curled in cups, like silver fog.
You screamed.

The fox's teat slipped out of his mouth—thick as a grub,
Spraying the floor white.

Maria Kardel

Aleppo boy

It's bound to leave a mess, the small thing with singed paper for skin,
trailing ash and blood like the other careless brats of its kind.
Sterile white walls and spotless orange cabinets frown at it
but at least it won't be here long, not with its decaying toes
barely hanging off the chair's edge, hair greyer than its mother
could dream of. Filthy scrounging blood clings to its withered face and
seals one eye, while the other, dull and black, stares into nothing,
towards nothing.

Even then, the picture of it leaves a stain. Unfortunate,
aimless thing, can't manage to keep the colour of its cheap shirt
from fading beneath dust. A cut-out from an old photograph
propped up on now's mantelpiece, touching where it shouldn't,
pressing marks in it. How foolish, thinking it can sit back
in our hard-earned civilisation.

Semsinur Kaya

Everything not saved
will be lost

There are a billion complex reasons behind your simplicity;
we live out each our own ellipsis.
A calaca swallowed by snakeskin that shapeshifts into taped fists
posing makeshift, save chance face slips
for the snapshot front page print.
Clamber up the monkey-bars of DNA strands,
hike the new worn ladder in her tights,
mouth caressed by black widow legs on this stratosphere sized spider's web
criss-crossing chaos plot looped by connecting threads.
Silken silver absent lining, holes to let the light draw in
swing across a myriad of arachnid-men.

How sad; my role models were all spandex-clad.
Grappling in squared circles,
simpler apartheid morals.
Portly plumber boys easily controlled
by pushing the right buttons
and waggling joysticks, little changes
still scared of blank pages and expectations,
just a little less rewarding. No high score counter for
the unending inadvertence, the wear and tear of lingering,
these zoetropic ruminations,
and their resulting damage control.

Samuel Kendall

Sis

My sister turned thirteen today
the catalytic age when a lab rat may finally choose, to an extent,
its overbearing experiments. Moving on from playing the parent pastiche
to her own individual attractive prospect.

Familiar phase, detained like a rip-off Stretch Armstrong in a tug of war,
one side pulling for the oblivious past, the other for the woman she's becoming.
Get used to the Elastoplast bandaging. Nobody should blame her
for the moments when she can no longer hold herself together.

She's begun ornamenting her clothes with a tea-stained decoupage,
grisaille school skirt gradually receding. All grown up and ready to be broken.
Slowly beginning to understand the awfulness, no opening doors to strangers,
no walks home alone in the cool black night.

She keeps asking what the pills are for and I don't know what to say.
Our heads don't have a fire escape, or any means to sift the ostensible smokescreen.
Soon she'll be where I am now, perhaps having done the same crash dummy
graduation spot,
chain conveyor to melting pot. Some men will want her in walk-in refrigerators,

skinned white mouse for basilisks and boa constrictors. Few things can be crueller
than a teenager.
I can't save her from any result: the snare of possibility.
Things would be worse anyhow, were she locked in an armoured suit of amethyst.
I'm so sorry, in advance, for all that they will do.

Samuel Kendall

Blanche Heriot
(out after curfew)

fix your mind on his face,
every detail as it were the day before.
his hair uncombed; his parched, chapped lips
    pretend this kiss of cold brass between your thighs is his
    as your fingers close the clasp of your hands
    about the clapper's bearing,
    like they might have had you flung your arms about his neck.
    greet him. draw him down into the smother of your breasts
        and stifle his groan with your own body.
tonight the curfew bell makes no sound
    for he dangles on its rope,
    swings with the arms of the ringer,
    who now ascends the stairs, by the tap of
        footsteps on the wood, to ring you up.
        he flings you forward first, then back.
        you grasp him tight, obey the rhythm
until the third stroke brings collision between flesh and metal,
its singing turned a dull and heavy smack that cannot carry.
    it is coming, though you do not hear the clash of hooves
    against the cobbles of the town; all else distant, forgotten,
but the ache of breaking bones, your inward bleeding,
    and the thought of your love spilling down from the belfry,
    washing over him with a noiseless cry.

your voice echoes out in heavenly baritone
       is he saved? is he saved? is he saved?

Amy Kinsman

Necessity

feel our fingers laced together in the space between us
and imagine forty-eight ribs knit as a single torso;

three lungs between us swelling in unison;
a single heart straining as it beats for both,

failing even now in the sleep drawn over us as a blanket,
its chambers and valves such an imperfect mirror of themselves—

and i, by lottery of birth, gifted the larger part, the left side:
i cleanse your blood, i give you breath, i hold you closed.

you must know, somewhere in the parts we share,
in the darkness of closed eyelids, in our faltering rhythms,

that every ticking minute you claim is a stolen one of mine
recanted before judge and executioner as they trial your theft in absentia.

here in my bloodied hand the scalpel awaits decision,
poised to sever.

Amy Kinsman

Tesseract

just as a cube is to a square
and a tesseract is to a cube
so this evening with you is
to the song in my head
which searches on the wrong pavements
for its accidental notes
finding instead only fungible things
and lost as the travelling air
(in her slippers)

I bestow a buttery kiss on each eyelid
of the axis of doubt
you are everything
that I'm sure wasn't there yesterday

but the butterscotch flavour eludes me
and on the inside
we am a balcony
looking across at so much snow
humming and failing
to taste my half-remembered

after midnight
the origami palace we made is lost to us both
it's right there as it was before
but the portico and all those staircases
now look more like some deserted orchard
and the closing door of her bedroom
and the sacred emblem of our fearsome burning
tyres

James Lewis

Three fragments from
the *Symposium*

This (forgetful) body. This (dreaming) body. This proud flesh will not
acknowledge its fault lines, does not comprehend how to be something /
anything other than whole. The hole shot through, the Klein-bottle
manner of being-in-the-world where every surface is open & porous,
every surface is bare & soft and exposed to the blind sun & spring rain
and eyes, everywhere eyes open & porous. These (other) bodies.

*

If the last man on earth sat in his house, and there came a knock upon
the door, how could this be? It's a language problem. Whereof I cannot
speak. And the most frustrating thing, that the space left between us
is a lexical gap and I could not tell you even if I tried, even if I wanted to.
Whereof I cannot speak (I might live). A human being in the manner
of a calque, taking the problem and atomising, recombining. Wondering
what it means to write love notes to a body I never had.

*

Whilst still walking, talking. In the midst of life. I became a memorial
of myself that on occasion would flicker like a distant star, the occlusion
a reminder of another body in the blackness. A break in the delicate
conductive filigree of the anatomy, reduced to the smallest figments,
carefully labelled *cuneiform*, *clavicle*, *ischium*. The wire clots wound
throughout the veins, the thermoplastic pillars of the capillaries an
unfitting monument. Teaching nothing, knowing nothing, no-thing.

Alex Marsh

Ronseal

Four plastic crates.

A roll mat. Two dust sheets. Two
cuts of grey carpet. A spade.

A floor mop. A hoover box.
Christmas decorations (various).
Two hoovers.

DVDS (n=74).

A brown leather satchel. An old
diary. A bowling bag. Ronseal.

A chest of drawers. Two lamp
shades. Two kilner jars. An empty
Techniques box.

A George Foreman Grill.

Paint samples. Spare room paint.
Dining room paint. Sellotape.
Dismantled shelves. Disk lock.
Gardening gloves.

That fucking pouffe.

A bag of bags. A bag of pegs.

Hair clippers.
A dehumidifier. A disposable
barbecue.

Five clothes airers—tangled.

Will Mason

Autumn

I

step away from that hot dream / coiling snake in the desert, everything bleached
     and wake. The morning's tentative, tastes bitter, as if you've done this
before. Peel back the duvet, ruffle the lawn. The harvest's been burnished
     by one white eye; the red world sharpened on a cold whetstone. Open your
mouth to lick it clean, only to find dry cinnamon coating your teeth.

II

last night the moon turned the leaves to ten pence pieces. Pick them up,
magpie-sly;
     tuck the change into one pocket. The coat's threadbare (last winter wore
it thin) and still yawning after summer's sleep. Some silver coins slip through
and tumble down
     gift back to the ground / its ore and bone.

III

Loneliness:
     chimney smoke swallowed by the hungry night;
     all those hours folded in the linen closet.

Catriona McLean

Reap

Follow this one home, there's hop on his breath / the sour sniff of salted soil. A slow proud ship that veers from North he slips into the verge, and dies / hazard lights beat / metronome.

You once saw a sheep like this; gaping mouth drying out, the body pulped to grass and stone.

Something touches his temple / hallowed grey-matter shrine, reverberates down neural pylons, synapse bites / hollows the eyes / severs his connections /

Catriona McLean

Travelling

A tidal movement: being
salted, washed, then
re-submerged, until
to move becomes
a hot, sandy bliss
or a slow forgetting—
      the crackle of corn's dry jacket
      and sheets left to parch on the line.

Its raw as a nerve—
to be away from home,
and looked on
by so many windows.

Now you're a live wire trying
not to earth—
or be drawn down into dank soil
and birthed—
a fresh seed with garish dreams—
skinned meat—

this thing that you are / this lizard's tongue, flicking
while I'm parched in the desert with a mind like water
a mind like yours sees only black / and the lazy white sun
bleaches every thought it licks

Catriona McLean

The bear pit

The school bus is the emblem of social hierarchy in the modern world.
Gap-toothed, backpack clad, *Charlie had a pigeon* echoes through
the narrow aisles of a pocket-sized feudal system. Pack mentality.
Children are really untamed beasts. And Life becomes their tamer—
sucks the wildness from their calcium bones, cuts out their shining eyes,
and places dead spheres in their place.

Queen. Worker. Drone. The hive mind of a comprehensive school
is a tragically beautiful thing to behold. Those with older brothers
(or a BMX) hold the magnifying glass. The rest—the bespectacled,
the anaemic, the vertically challenged—are the ants. 'Stars, hide your
fires; Let not light see my black and deep desires.' That is: to staple
a packet of *Werther's Originals* to the class antagonist's skull.

At fourteen years old, every face is an open book. My eyes still looked
upon the world with wonder (not dread), socks pulled up to my knees,
life in the passenger seat. 'Spread your wild oats' my teacher said to me,
before I was old enough to understand what 'my oats' truly were or how
on earth I should go about spreading them.

Eleanor Murphy

Galaxies

We watched from the mezzanine,
the gathered crowds lighting fireworks,
bellowing their goodbyes with acronyms
and capitals—*a long road, love and hate.*
We bore witness the end of our own world,
the pixelated dragons and glitched armour,
the empty houses, alcoves laden with trophies.
We looked up from the fading sand—
other worlds where others gathered
beneath iron horses and green pyramids.
Some sat beneath towering trees, or alone,
in swamps, in snow, in ash and fire.
We counted together—farewells, a brief message,
and then, in a flicker—nothing. It was gone.
The all-nighters as hopeless undergrads,
the itch while backpacking in summer,
the gentle rise of the welcoming refrain—
I hear it still, on quiet nights, when screens are dark.
There was a day I stood in that place that doesn't exist—
I walked, out beyond the sandstone walls,
out beyond the desert steppes—
it was still there, deep within the valley of bones,
as if untouched by greed it stood, clear and bright.
I sat before the doorway, and looked upon the empty tracts.
Will you return? I promise.
Those were the last words we spoke.

James O'Sullivan

A lover's plea?

Along a street in the sky,
A man, thirteen storeys up,
Leaned over and sprayed:
'I love you will u marry me.'

The graffiti stays high above the city
Visible for miles,
Yelling at the top of its voice.
Is it a lover's plea?

Now neon overlaps those words,
Those words that were once
Fading into the concrete.
The note, now, depersonalised.

This act of vandalism
Transformed into an iconic landmark,
A universal message
Declaring the optimism of love.

Written during ThinkCreate, the Faculty of
Arts and Humanities' core interdisciplinary
module.

Charlie John Pashley

Only simplify

a sea rolling high
STC

Just simple words, a simple voice and its feeling, green common on which
to feed, shaft of mote-light through my glass transparency, and where did
my lover go, and why did he go and leave me, here alone with thorn and
babe, beneath blind Skiddaw's oblivious height, chaste moon shining on
my greedy appetite, hunger of the sense, for me and mine and nature's
power, calm and equable and contained, do you hear that echo 'mid the
shouting birds?, do you see with your eye the shattering cataract's still
and fearful majesty?, self o self in prayer meditation composition, light of
the heart received and given, words' vision, freeholder's dream, the giant
child with his elemental monstrous daddy in the mountains, rocks,
streams and lakes, have you seen the owl a-hooting so, the pastoral lambs
a-skipping-o, mighty voice, mightier mind, self-creating, self-sustaining,
low as the mole in ages dug, high as the sky-lark's hover 'tween matter-of-
fact old earth and palace-heights of cloud, do you not sense the brooding
of the dove, with Milton's burr over waters clear as Shakspear's heart?,
England, spiritual, sensuous, passionate, beating with the ancient loping
pulse along the incarnadine rivers of the blood, France, abstract, manic,
morbid, running with tyrannical rivers of blood, o my memory, court of
noble kings, the Moses of my understanding, the Druid of my primitive
faith, the gawky boy with the immortal slouch, the mad old woman who
still cannot speak, the tender pastor under dripping trees, the two
strange Friends who laid on kindly hands, the garrulous knight with the
generous purse, I am a man and little else amongst my solid dreams of
companionship, country roads that end, like lines do end, in infinite
white, violent visions on an empty mountain-top, woman and man hand
in hand along the genial lake-bright way, and all besides the imagining
mind, intense with nature, sees its ghost, like the shadow of colossus,
dark against the mounting clouds, accompanied by substantial grace,
insubstantial feeling simple as the heart before the lingering dawn.

The old man stumbles amongst ragwort and celandine, mud in his eye as
the Duddon flows laughing by.

Adam Piette

looking out over

off out
        staring over the roads
by the way
        i was staring out off
into the distance, looking pushed up against the laundry
so cold
        that it felt wet even when rubbed close up into the face
& i try every time to remember that just because it's purple it doesn't
mean it smells like lavender
sit awhile
        in the garden by the ivy on the breaking
wall and wonder
what it breathes in twilight
        thrown back against the smooth linoleum smearing cooling
droplets together against my skin sticking with hot wet water my
whole world in a giggly blur
and twilight
        sitting down gathering in orange
cold, cold,
        gathering up skirts and garters—lace is a half baked dream to me,
he's broken
soaring somewhere else in twilight and yet my hands
                                looping
back around
at me   looping

and wait   looping
     standing   in the kitchen dark, sailor legged and lonely
                                    just
the way i like

Harper S

After the eclipse

The Sun perished slowly, almost
As if it were reluctant; as if, after
Four-point-six billion years alight,
It didn't want to leave,
Not even for a moment. I watched
Through wise and wicked lenses, saw
The Promethean flame, the Aztec god,
Consumed by an incongruous darkling edge
That seemed to me like cancer, with its
Subtle yet implacable advance. The tumour
Swelled as daylight died, feasting on the lamp
Of life, humiliating physics and our human self-importance.
Birdsong faded; in its place
My ragged lonely breath—louder
Than *The Last Post* on the eleventh of November—
Made meagre mourning. Who was I
To take the last breath of the world? And so
I held it, feeling, though in weaker form, the
Solar giant's suffering, as it and I were slowly
Starved to death. I felt
My energy devoured by a midnight veil
Of malice, the creeping shadow of entropy
Fall upon my face, and I was cold, so cold
That Icarus could stroke my cheek and still
His wax would hold. The land was grey, and
Nothing glinted, glowed or glittered, but sucked
In light; every blade of grass
Possessed the greedy gravity of infinite mass.
No funeral was held that day,
And not a soul wore black;
Like fools, we all believed it would come back.

Aaron Saint John

Dating

Describe me the same way
all West Country want-to-be-guitar-men do.
Like a field. Bloody lush, beautiful.
I'll try making the most of happy.

Last week
we tried to reach the water,
fishermen only.
I used to wake up early on Saturdays
before my swimming lessons
knock on your bedroom door
and walk straight in
it was broken, the handle.
I saw something in the mirrored wardrobe
I shouldn't.
My body rejected water after that.

Pulled under a type of tide
twice I broke the doctor's back
with my non-muscles.
A scream for Mother, not you
not you.
I told her she was just like you
that was the worst thing ever said.

Yesterday
your reflection was on West Street
by the time I spat you'd evaporated.
A stranger snaps the straps off me later
that brings us up to date.

Katie Rose Smart

Not quite midnight

He pisses in his boxers and ties them in a Sainsbury's carrier
—one from before the 5p charge—flimsy. Thrown into the unmown,
amongst the unrust; slides and swings and things.
This time attempted asphyxiation was meant to keep the boxers quiet
its fly shut, hush. They wish it was their head in the bag.
A strange pumpkin looking thing hits the ground
and exhales for the first time since he walked in.
Looking for glass clues
finding them emptied.

Katie Rose Smart

Curation texts:

#1 The nuisance of capturing dreams

The nuisance of capturing dreams / Britain has slipped thru the sense of itself. You can only see it when you leave it. Like once I went to / this is too grand / I saw Thracian caves cracked open by centuries of Black Sea earthquakes, golden heat. And this is too grand / but subsidence quakes through the coalfields again. Subsidence flashes new lakes. To forget is primordial, water-borne / remember, and life is tough / the monuments their latest allowance of that. Collection buckets shake with coppers for the disaster monument / a bronze widow saddled with a bruised toddler / a bandstand by a purpose / *a whiter shade of pale* dissembling brass into its drone / clatters its campaign upon the breeze / from the drought of time that drained its rehearsal emerge hearts which never had to practise / dim efficiencies to hold us   like metres of faint poems

#2 Wrong things

that trouble me since Brexit. Mistakes are sudden, plummet one / anything goes / knuckles out of numbness for the Poles / on the TV, a party conference calls jobs *British* / then the American maternity invoice which itemised skin-to-skin contact, post-caesarean, at $39.35 / since drinking daily into / longer happy / longer lucid / longer thinner states / dealing with it, but what can you say that isn't an itemising? Talking in poetry: the more elegant, the more valuable its print / once familial love in contact is itemised as a new commodity / twice into its poetic apocalypse / at least $39.35 still has corners and sides, at least paper and coin / Invert the transaction: how much pain for the main items of news? Emaciation's latest ribs / cannulae clogged and powdered with plaster / elbows pinning their last embrace / the bewildered boy in the ambulance bay / the Syria rotating through our bedrooms / life as the awe at no end till some next time   still we write

Bryn Tales

This side of the city

'For there's more enterprise / in walking naked.'
WB Yeats

On this side of the city home is like losing parents
to dementia, they touch the curved arms
 of an IKEA chair and know it's a different country
but they live with habitual non-memory
of *Nowrooz*, *yalda*, *ghorme sabzi*,
even the coldness in their feet never
remind them of the heat under the *korsi*.

Some cities have borderline designs, there is a car park
on Milton Street that turns into a drive-in cinema
where apathetic cars watch the young Travolta
dancing in Grease, but the rest of the year
it is the finishing point of a long stare as if it was the Caspian Sea,

they say 'once upon a time there was a hole in the road,'
the one I never saw in real world, it's the same void that degenerates
the mind, a hole in the definition of the town, like having to mime
to estranged thoughts, and again, 'what's the big fuss?'
asks a Sheffield lad with little loyalty to his mother's or the city's past,

on this side of the city Sunday afternoon yawns
in a dodgy lift in an unloved brutalist building
cramped with immigrants, in an immigrant home family
is an embroidered word you can throw on a sofa
and binge-watch foreign language series, subtitled psychobabbles
about actually nothing, about how one can be busy
all Sunday afternoon moving from one madness to another,
from mother to father.

They say a rose survives longer if you insert a needle
into the stem and let go the air, how many holes are enough
to let go the drifting thoughts that have yet to settle?
What if the needles, like memories, go blind
and shred the wrong place in the wrong time?

They say stories are rotating circles that touch each other,
perhaps somewhere on the other side of the city,
in that overlapped space, we redesign the borders,
invent a language, display our wounds, walk *naked*,
and tell the others we haven't survived, we only fake it.

Shirin Teifouri

The lower lake

i

The summer is past, the schools are full.
The sky is a cut peach.
Through the humidity
the fat man rows, heaped like spoil in his row-boat,
struggling the water and air. You
are swimming lengths through the cold
drawn
under-water of the reservoir,
the tannin silk, the rot.
Lifeguards, college girls browned and red-wrapped
gather on the raked sand
to jostle their sharp perfections.

ii

The sun sets itself down like a sack among the hills,
a charcoal stump, a bright trickle
for the gullies. The brook
carries on, assuming the lake
portion by portion. Cavalcade of shadows. You
have laced yourself
tightly together, buried the ends, promised yourself again
to the difficulty,
as among the darkened lily stems
perch are busy
piecing together the over-perch, the one thought worth thinking
for perch.

iii

Oblivion of crickets
over the black baskets of trees, the watchtower air, the settled miles.
There are trains
moving, heavy bells among the boughs. There are roots
and lures, nests
cracking
in the willows. You
are warm in the dark with yourself—
the granite ciphers, the quarries of sleep. I too
and for twenty years have drifted these woods. I am more than nothing to them,
a try of their pollen,
a summer stem of their perfection.

iv

Early light let from the pines and night
put away in its pots. Catbirds tinker in the filaments
of lilac. Slight ruin
beneath the trellised grapes—the scabrous table, the still tea.
The vines
have climbed to the mock-orange, are reaching
for the dogwood
and are themselves a trellis for honeysuckle.
Mothers linger at the street corner, the lit grapes
are crowded with darkness and you
are a brook
of blood, that difficult water.

David Troupes

The Arkaquah trail

The labourers gone home, the scaffolds bare
and fluttering—evening
piles down, and the scaffolds

stay
while the world falls away. Rags
and rubble-throats, ribways of rhododendron,

veins and spines of the ridge. The walker walks
the bouncing planks, pauses, pulls
from pipe to pipe—

no sense of report, no sense
of return—above an April residue
of blossom and church, among

the squalling sun, the evening snows—
hurrying
like a word toward its tongue.

David Troupes

How to find your way in the dark

It was so soon after I arrived in the city
The venue's scent an orange light
Rock dispersed by amps
Posters of faces, a cymbal-heart topology, waves of thudding ink
Everyone knowing the same words differently

And it was winter, the sky light, cut, thin
What I should have brought I didn't, my hands volcanoes
Finding it hard to breathe, harder to write, impossible to dream
The challenges seemed
To toughen with the callouses
And the chords weren't dissonant
Just perishing

At this stage I didn't know you at all
Like everyone
The smoking area sky clear like the back of a hand
Scattered dumpsters a frog song tableau
The night's spilt drinks
Half-drawn stars and glowing
But we were still speaking when the light faded to ruby
When it highlighted the world in green

Do you remember the moth that landed on your cheek?
You were telling the difference
Between RAM and ROM
The space that motherboards leave
For time

As vacant as dawn
In a different city
Busy and lost
Finding out, again and again, the parity
Of cig ends
And the burning burning Moon

Joe Vaughan

The split-palm steeple: a confession

I like you best with smear of jam on cheek
(to be married by the hair strands)
A raspberry line that bends with the unripe croaks of daybreak
asking if I have watered our prayer plant:

'It is quenched' I say,
            though by my touch
                        and not the can.

                                    The velvet veins,
                        whisping in moonlight
            crying out for soft strokes.

Back and forth,
            petiole postulate—
                        The soiree and sway,

                                                                        your lips at
                        the dinner table
            pushed out as if the air is a magnet   repelled by the sun-split hour

So hush,
            (please rob them of ornament)
                        and place, (honest now)
                                                                        like the velvet
                        one
                        upon our mantelpiece,   one leaf
            crumbled*

            *An accidental hoover suck, my sincerest apologies

Evie Wilson

Men in sheds

The men in sheds are at it again
blossoming in confession like petal tablets on the tongue

They do it in secret
When the sky is cloaked with grey
(For they thrive in competition)

All it takes is an axe in palm
perhaps a ball on foot
for the truth to ricochet

And we see it on his face
the curving of his spine
like a fetus
or a black dog
or a cloud
(filled with tears)

Evie Wilson

Ockham's razors

(I) The bath tub is a vessel,   like an ornament, a bobble?*

    when reversed   magnet, so sweet

    it protests its negotiation.   from our mouths'

        We push it

        like death wish
      And murmur on meniscus
    (II)* to graze our bubbling lips

        should full

    but not   the crib it

(III) As if like   put to sleep.

Evie Wilson

Rousseau and his minds

Some people are
simply born to be at
nature's top table,
it's teaching them
manners that's the
problem, to pass the
mutton without
being asked, to
warm the cheese for
all to savour, to make
wine the prize of wit,
let the world war
only in words.

Wake up, wake up, wake up!
Where's your fire inside?
There's a revolution in town
wearing silk stockings looking
lika a prince taking a stroll,
how can you know you
what you need if you
have not thought about
what you wear? Wake up!
Dress your mind.

I'm coming to see I have a
tricky side, I'm coming to
see there's a problem with
money, I'm coming to see
that I'm going to have to
separate my words, some
for you and some for me,
but all for sale at the right
price, a man has to eat
after all.

You really don't want to know
what it's like to see perfection
as I do out the corner of my
right eye, that sits at the edge of
reason and personification of
love, which I add, is an exact
thing, just a matter
of arranging the notes, the
order of which
is known to me upon
sight of you: who are you but
my means to a song?

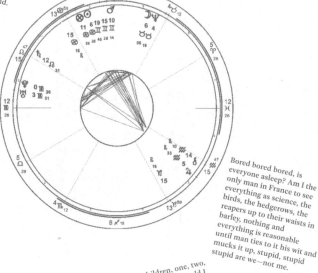

Bored bored bored, is
everyone asleep? Am I the
only man in France to see
everything as science, the
birds, the hedgerows, the
reapers up to their waists in
barley, nothing and
everything is reasonable
until man ties to it his wit and
mucks it up, stupid, stupid
stupid are we—not me.

What of my children, one, two,
three, four, five? What would I
know? It's their world, not mine.

Margot Wilson

Faulkner's private eye

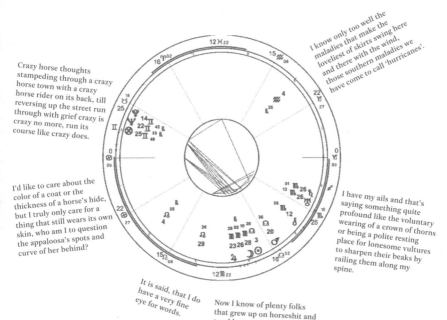

Crazy horse thoughts stampeding through a crazy horse town with a crazy horse rider on its back, till reversing up the street run through with grief crazy is crazy no more, run its course like crazy does.

I know only too well the maladies that make the loveliest of skirts swing here and there with the wind, those southern maladies we have come to call 'hurricanes'.

I'd like to care about the color of a coat or the thickness of a horse's hide, but I truly only care for a thing that still wears its own skin, who am I to question the appaloosa's spots and curve of her behind?

I have my ails and that's saying something quite profound like the voluntary wearing of a crown of thorns or being a polite resting place for lonesome vultures to sharpen their beaks by railing them along my spine.

It is said, that I do have a very fine eye for words.

Now I know of plenty folks that grew up on horseshit and tumbleweed and killers for a pa and mam, but I grew up on the refinement of self-discipline accompanied by the mind's charm to read between the lines and show the making of a whore is just the wrongness in a man's mind, I'm not to be fussing over misleading detail that frees you from the toils of my stories, made yours by the forgetting start of each sentence that goes on and on, why, I've made you go on a calamitous ride where tumbleweed and horseshit feel like home sweet home.

Margot Wilson

Por la tarde—Choluteca

12 pm

Arid and black rooster
Vulture-clustered roadside
Gizzard-face dogs finish.
Fruit stalls of black banana,
Grey orange, gold tooth,
Bags of beans, shoeless kids
Burn plastic to the sun.

1 pm

The ants spew from their baking cracks
Resume a sack of bar limes
Almost steaming by the road.
Deftly part the dust and rind
From their last grip on juice.
It never rains this time of year
But may break this afternoon.

2 pm

Narrow dogsballs swinging in the shade
(the ants would love to get at these)
beneath their emaciated formings of bone.
Trotting with long leather tongues
Lace-worked in wound skins
With promise latent
Of vegetal moisture.

3 pm

In the kitchen I smell melon:
A nice dozen pile the floor,
An orgy of dozing tortoise
                          On tile.
In the afternoon heat, their shells
Split shatter their backs
Shower their juices.
                     Insides bloom.

4 pm

Between the flowers newly browned
One notes correspondingly
The smell they impart growing
As heat rises from the dead petal,
The backbone of the mountains,
And disperses in the clouds.
Wind blows leaves through the patio.

5 pm

An hour of light
Through the various cross-hatchings:
A wood-wickered rocking chair,
A man-eating hammock,
The tallest tree to the west.
Birds slowly circle the sky.
Voice-less. Name-less.

6 pm

The wind is up, the power's down
And one walks slow
            To keep the candle burning
With gritty feet sliding
            Round the creaking kitchen.
Underground, the water in the cistern
            Is still warm.

Dominic Zugai

Editors

Rachel Zerihan
Zelda Hannay

of voices aiming to be read, by you, by the writer in you, by the imagination that lives on language which only art can coax into delightful attention. With thanks to all the editors, to Matthew and his team and to Go! Grafik. And an especial thanks to the writers who took the risk and stepped into the public arena of print: what an issue this is, a book to be proud of.

Prof Adam Piette
School of English

Writers

Poetry
Ben Allen
Chad Bentley
Simon Broomhead
Sam Buchan-Watts
Joe Caldwell
Grace Cohen
Mara-Daria Cojocaru
Frederick Coombes
John Darley
Kristina Diprose
Jenny Donnison
Peter S Dorey
Veronica Fibisan
Jack Field
Pete Green
Ali Hayward
Jenny Hockey
Gary Hughes
Aidan Jenner
Maria Kardel
Semsinur Kaya
Samuel Kendall
Amy Kinsman
James Lewis
Alex Marsh
Will Mason
Catriona McLean
Eleanor Murphy
James O'Sullivan
Charlie John Pashley
Adam Piette
Harper S
Aaron Saint John

Katie Rose Smart
Bryn Tales
Shirin Teifouri
David Troupes
Joe Vaughan
Evie Wilson
Margot Wilson
Dominic Zugai

Performance
Stephen Chase
Ethan Freestone
Miriam Schechter

Fiction
Chad Bentley
Emily Elizabeth France
Lucy Hamilton
Jenna Muiderman
Aaron Saint John
Rebecca Sandeman
Maria Vegro
Samuel Wadkin
Leanne Williams
Dominic Zugai

Non-Fiction
Emily-Rose Baker
Peter S Dorey
Carolina Kylimann
The Radical Theory
   Collective
Eleanor Slater
Anne Temple Clothier

Library music

for any number of readers of Route 57:

read your copy of *Route 57* methodically following page sequence
(start / stop anywhere) or dip in at will

for every word beginning or ending with the following five letters,
a corresponding action:

R

raise book and hold horizontally over a table about five, seven,
35, 57, 285 or 399 centimetres high and drop to land flat on a table

O

blow across page edges once: single pages, groups of pages, pages loose or
closed / compressed together, vary intensity of breath and page compression
(play in combination with E if word begins / ends o ... e or e ... o)

U

hold spine edge and flap / wobble pages for five or seven seconds

T

place book on a flat surface with fingers of one hand positioned on upper
part of front cover, fingers of other hand on lower half and propel the book
in circular fashion widdershins or deasil

E

flick once through pages of book—explore differing speeds

ad lib:
- once or twice during the course of the piece turn to any page and read
  aloud—calmly and deliberately—every fourth, sixth, ninth, tenth,
  fourteenth, fifteenth, 21st, 22nd, 25th, 26th, 33rd, 34th, 35th, 38th, 39th,
  46th, 49th, 51st, 55th, 57th word
- make a short *shh* sound on identifying the sound of two or more
  simultaneous sounds relating to this score; over the course of a
  performance start to elongate your *shh* sounds, making them
  correspondingly softer each time

(if performing in a library take care not to unduly disturb your fellow patrons).

Stephen Chase

Three pieces taken from a collection of 50+ scores called *outofdoors suite* (2011–present). Simple ideas with simple / complex results to be played individually or in sequences in the middle of nowhere or a bustling city by any number of people who are so minded to try them.

Fred & Ginger piece

in a group in an echoic space (eg alleyway) compare and contrast the sounds of each of your footsteps—quality of shoe clatter on surfaces, pace and phrasing of walking—notice how each sets off its own particular set of reflections—try various sequences and simultaneous combinations

(optional: should you encounter an abandoned trolley near an alleyway, push it at speed through the alley—you may yodel Tarzanstyle as you do this)

Stephen Chase

Phoning it in

should you have a mobile phone and encounter a public telephone box, take note of the number

start walking away from the box stopping occasionally to call the number

see how far from the box you can walk before the ringing of the phone becomes inaudible

observe, listen

if the phone is answered you may engage in a conversation

Stephen Chase

Whistle while you walk

listening

sometimes whistling

whilst out walking

by yourself or with others

a single whistled tone
every twenty or more steps
(sometimes many more)

variously short and up to a full breath
keep an ear out for hockets,[1] chords, beats,[2] etc.

relaxed, rarely that loud

a melody (melodies) in slow motion

guided by feel of embouchure, resonance of location, other pitches heard

1   A rapid alternation of notes between performers
    creating a fragmented melodic line.
2   Acoustic interference between two closely
    (mis)tuned tones.

Stephen Chase

Dios es Julia

Dios es Julia is taken from a set of songs called Light the match, *which follows the story of a conflicted soldier, Sebastian, and a local woman, Julia, from a small war torn town. The story follows their internal struggles and documents their chance meeting, leading Sebastian to desert and elope with Julia, and eventually face the consequences of his actions.*

For a solitary female voice, with a slow rhythm and mostly in a minor key.

Like a plaster trying to cover up a bullet hole
Like a pat on the shoulder trying to fix a broken soul
There's no mending what she's missing
No pretending, she's stopped wishing
No way out of this hellish burial ground

[Chorus]
Lord, it's Julia
Are you listening, are you watching?
Do you see the state my fragile head is in?

My faith is shaking, world is breaking
Are you watching, are you watching?
I can only live for so long on adrenaline

Like a letter after earthquakes rip the world apart
Like a warning not to begin after she already starts
Self destruction doesn't help her
But the crying overwhelms her
When every spark of light has been drowned

[Chorus]
Lord, it's Julia
Are you listening, are you watching?
Do you see the state my fragile head is in?
My faith is shaking, world is breaking
Are you watching, are you watching?
I can only live for so long on adrenaline

Like a ray of hope that can't break through the clouds
One more happy thought is brutally shot down
She wants to leave, to get away
But instead she's forced to stay
Trapped inside the place she once called home

[Bridge]
Lord, it's Julia
I can't help but feel ignored
Do you see me?
Can you hear me?
What do I have to do?
Please tell me what to do

[Chorus]
Lord, it's Julia
Are you listening, are you watching?
Do you see the state my fragile head is in?
My faith is shaking, world is breaking
Are you watching, are you watching?
I can only live for so long on adrenaline

Lord, it's Julia
Are you listening, are you watching?
I'm thinking I might have to pack it in
My faith is shaking, while I'm still waiting
I'm debating, contemplating
But I'm failing, life is draining
Are you listening, are you listening?
I can only live for so long on adrenaline

Ethan Freestone

Blackbird,
Scene 2

HENRY is a dishevelled young man who in the previous scene had his hand stolen by a blackbird who is using it to become a famous pianist. In this scene, HENRY begins to forget that his hand has been stolen.

Only a table and chair are present on stage.

WAITER: Hello, what can I get you?

HENRY: Nothing, thank you.

HENRY tries to get up, but WAITER keeps him down.

WAITER: You're waiting for your friend, aren't you?

HENRY: No. I'm just looking for a blackbird.

WAITER: Then why did you tell me before that you're waiting for your friend? Anyway, you have to order something or you can't stay here.

HENRY: I don't want to stay here.

WAITER: Sure you do. What can I get you?

HENRY: Nothing.

WAITER: Come on now, less of this. I'll bring you a bowl of olives.

HENRY: But then what if my friend comes, and I'm stuffing my face? I'd have olive everywhere. I might burp! What if I get full and then fill myself up and when my friend comes, I have to eat another meal and then get so stuffed that my trouser button comes undone and it hits her straight in the eye?

WAITER: Oh dear. Do you know when your date is going to arrive? The other customers are complaining that you look lonely.

HENRY: It's a date?

WAITER: No, I won't go on a date with you!

HENRY: I mean now... am I waiting for a date?

WAITER: I believe so—you're all nervous and sweaty and have only ordered olives.

HENRY: I'm not only nervous and sweaty when I'm waiting for a date. There are other times too.

WAITER: Probably. You seem like you're one of those people who gets nervous and sweaty even when you don't need to be nervous and sweaty. Like when a bomb goes off or you're about to go in for a job interview.

HENRY: Yes, I do get nervous and sweaty then too.

WAITER: See.

HENRY: I'm getting even more nervous and sweaty now.

WAITER: How fast is your heart beating?

HENRY: Probably at about the speed of a caterpillar on top of a cheetah.

WAITER: That's quite fast. Should I call the doctor?

HENRY: No!

WAITER: Why not?

HENRY: I'm going later anyway.

WAITER: Why?

HENRY: I forgot.
WAITER: You forgot your doctor and you forgot your date. You must be one of those people with upside down ears.
HENRY: That's not true at all!
WAITER: Prove it.
HENRY: I can't and I shan't.
WAITER: Why not?
HENRY: It's too hot. My ears are probably all nervous and sweaty and if you looked at them they might have a panic attack.
WAITER: That wouldn't be very good for business.
HENRY: Are you going to bring me those olives?
WAITER: I suppose, but are you going to give me your nose?
HENRY: Definitely not. I need it for show.
WAITER: It's not even that nice anyway. All round and it's got two holes in it! I don't even think I want it after all.
HENRY: Well you've got your own anyway.
WAITER: Yes, but every now and again things get caught up it and I have to fish them out with a spade and a bucket. I think it's faulty.
HENRY: Maybe *you* should go to the doctor.
WAITER: Me?
HENRY: Yes, you. About your nose.
WAITER: Oh, I thought you were talking about my toes. I've only got six you know. Dropped the other ones down the sink.
HENRY: I could make you some out of napkins as replacement?
WAITER: That won't do. I might get all nervous and sweaty one day and the napkins would disintegrate.
HENRY: Or soak it all up.
WAITER: Soak what up?
HENRY: The sweat.
WAITER: I think you produce far too much sweat from being all nervous and sweaty for just a little napkin to soak up. You probably need to walk around with a paddling pool underneath you.
HENRY: Don't you think that that may get funny looks?
WAITER: With a nose like that you probably already get funny looks. *(raucous laughter)*
HENRY: Oh. Could you bring the olives now? What colour do you have?
WAITER: Pink.
HENRY: Pink olives? They're my least favourite...
WAITER: Perfect then. I'll bring them right away.

> WAITER exits. Righthanded piano music plays. HENRY is intrigued to where it is coming from. He looks under the chairs and table.

HENRY: Isn't that strange? That music? It sounds like — *(cut off by WAITER entering loudly)*
WAITER: No pink olives. Only yellow. Will have to do.
HENRY: But yellow olives are my most favourite!
WAITER: What a disaster this is. *(collapses onto the floor in tears)* I really can't do anything right for this restaurant.
HENRY: Look, what sort of restaurant is this anyway? I've been here for hours. And my watch was working fine yesterday and now I can't find it anywhere.

WAITER: Have you looked under the table?
HENRY: That's where I looked for the music.
WAITER: What music?
HENRY: The music that was playing earlier. I thought it was hiding under the table.
WAITER: *(kindly)* Music doesn't hide under tables.
HENRY: I didn't think so either.
WAITER: So why did you look there?
HENRY: I think I was looking for my watch.
WAITER: You have to stop losing things under the table in my restaurant. It's bad for business. The other customers just told me that you're ruining their meal.
HENRY: How?
WAITER: You're lonely. And nervous. And sweaty. Also they think it's unfortunate that you're wearing a nose with two holes in it.
HENRY: None of those things are anything that I can help!
WAITER: What a shame, because they're paying customers and you're not.
HENRY: I could be a paying customer.
WAITER: You haven't paid me yet. Not with anything. *(makes a gesture that HENRY could pay him with a sexual favour)*
HENRY: *(getting up in horror)* I don't know if I have anything to pay you with.
WAITER: Seems to me that you've got a problem.
HENRY: I'll leave then!

HENRY tries to leave but is stopped by WAITER.

WAITER: Oh no, no no no. We'll talk about that later. We'll need your chair in a minute.
HENRY: Well even better for me to leave and then you can have it.
WAITER: No. We need it warm and fresh.
HENRY: Why?
WAITER: There's a couple in the restaurant about to have a baby.
HENRY: A baby?
WAITER: Don't you know what a baby is? You used to be one, you know. So did I.
HENRY: Prove it.
WAITER: You see this mark over here, on my elbow?
HENRY: Yes.
WAITER: Well then, I've proven it.
HENRY: No you haven't.
WAITER: *(angrily)* You are a FUCKING a nightmare. Look, we need your chair now. Your date isn't even here yet.

HENRY and WAITER start to fight over the chair.

HENRY: You can't take my chair. There are chairs over there!
WAITER: No, those won't do. The people who sat on them previously were having a midlife crisis so we're going to have to burn them. It's policy.
HENRY: Well my date will be here any second now.
WAITER: Sir, the couple, they're about to have a baby! They need your chair.
HENRY: Wouldn't they much prefer to hold their baby?
WAITER: No! They want to finish their meal.

WAITER and HENRY get very angry fighting over the chair.
HENRY sees that WAITER is very upset so gives it up.

HENRY: Oh, well can I have it back afterwards?

WAITER: Certainly. We will wipe it down and bring it straight back. The baby is set to have ten fingers, twelve toes, and a little splatter of ketchup on its bottom! Aren't babies cute?

HENRY: I wouldn't know, I've never held one.

WAITER: You've never held a baby?

HENRY: I don't want to.

WAITER: *(drops the chair)* You're an awful person.

HENRY: You don't know that.

WAITER: Yes, I do.

> *Right handed piano music plays for the rest of the scene until WAITER sits down. The music reminds HENRY that his hand has been stolen from him. The music taunts him.*

HENRY: Wait. What was I here for again?

WAITER: Sir. We need your chair.

HENRY: You can have it.

WAITER: I don't need it yet.

HENRY: Something happened.

WAITER: You're just waiting for your date.

HENRY: No. You're lying. There was something else.

WAITER: Nothing else. Just the olives.

HENRY: You're distracting me! Shut up.

WAITER: *(a little scared)* How about a glass of wine? You're clearly nervous and sweaty. It will calm you.

HENRY: No. Stop it.

WAITER: Your chair is over here, sir.

HENRY: You should really stop this.

WAITER: Come on now, sit down.

HENRY: *(copying WAITER and shouting into his face)* Come on now, sit down. Come on now, sit down.

> *WAITER sits down on the table.*

HENRY: *(to WAITER)* Who are you?

WAITER: *(WAITER seems to forget their whole previous conversation)* Who are you?

HENRY: What was I here for?

WAITER: What were you here for?

HENRY: *(getting increasingly louder, angrier, and more scared)* What did I come here for? Where is that music coming from?

> *HENRY pushes the table to the corner with WAITER on top of it.*

WAITER: What are you doing?

HENRY: Stop it, I can't think!

> *Music stops abruptly. WAITER sits down.*

HENRY: My hand... where did I put it? I distinctly remember using it to brush my teeth with this morning. *(to the audience)* Hey, do you know where I left it?

Miriam Schechter

FICTION

Editors

Stephanie Dando
Kristina Wearing
Lucy Hamilton
Aysha W Musa
Upamanyu Das
Emily Elizabeth France
Eleanor N Slater
Kevin Fox
Melanie Smiley
Nicola Hodson

Have you ever?

'Have you ever—told a Lie?'
Samantha's voice plugged the circle like a damper stuffed into a saxophone.

The girls swivelled from Leah to survey the new speaker. Samantha's question had had its desired effect; the circle was once again hers.

But Samantha's own eyes were fixed soundly on Leah, the menace in her smirk like the tip of knife between shoulder blades. Leah stayed silent. Samantha had meant for that too.

The other girls continued to stare, their itching impatience now scratched by Samantha's inter-jection. The lick of her 'L' still wet on their lobes, the shrillness of her vowel still sharp in their ears, Leah's shy dithering now forgotten.

Katie was the first to break the silence.

'Told a Lie?!' She gawped, 'I've never!'

A pause and then 'Have you, Ky?'

Kylie shook her head.

Their two frowning faces mirrored each other for a moment before swinging back around to face Samantha. Her full, crescent lips sucked lightly on the rim of her bottle, drinking in their attention. Slowly, deliberately, she up-tipped her hand, forcing the liquid to creep up the neck, enjoying the chink of her teeth on the glass and the amplified fizz as the foam resettled. Kylie's eyes slipped to the floor, but all thoughts of the game lay scattered like the circle of cards in the centre.

Opposite, Katie was equally stunned. Her eyes kept flicking to the glow of the blinker pulsing above the shutters, its sharp red vigilance dulled by the polythene sheet that Samantha had stolen and they'd fixed over the lens. Stealing was one thing. Stealing was forgivable. But this...

She looked back at Katie and together their lips slowly curled. None of them ever had, now

Samantha had to tell her full story; that was the rule of their game. Kylie glanced up again but the pulse remained constant. Their gathering still secret, they wouldn't be overheard. And yet, Samantha leaned in a little closer. They mirrored her, eager for the details, when another voice uttered,

'I have.'

A grey, inked-message burned beneath a sleeve at the memory.

'What?'

Leah nodded. Her letters on her wrist flared again.

'*You've* told a Lie?' Katie's wide eyes turned orbicular, the casual tone of her dismissal exposing how often they snubbed Leah when she wasn't there. Leah felt a pang; though she knew it already, the brash reminder stung. But the slight disappeared like a paper cut beneath the acid of Samantha's disdain. She glared at her challenger, unblinking, her slick, glossy mane framing her face like bars of a prison cell, crooked and bent. Leah was forced to look away.

She stared down at the floor as though littered with the words she'd just spilled and rubbed her wrist against her thigh, relieving the itch on the inside of her sleeve. She prayed the other girls wouldn't notice—they might mistake it for an attempt to conceal the real agony they'd be warned of but could only imagine; when the inked letters burned on the wrist of a Liar, a reminder of the value of honesty. They might think her confession was a Lie in itself and that would be worse than the truth.

The truth that she shouldn't have spoken. She wished that she hadn't. But in Samantha's dark eyes,

Leah had glimpsed something glistening in the depth
and had bitten down, hard. The surgical glint of a hook.
She could taste the oily mass in the back of her throat.

Steel tugged at her tongue.

'Only once,' murmured Leah, 'but I have.'

Kylie's wine glass was suspended mid-air, collecting
their thoughts, the eddying questions. The glass
slipped a little in her fingers.

'Wow,' she managed, awestruck.

Gently, Leah slid her arm further inside her sleeve
until only the very tips of the letters were visible.
Though the ink looked no different and still felt cool
to the touch, Leah felt sure that Samantha would
find a way to make the others see a change, even when
it wasn't there. Leah didn't want to tempt her.

'Wow,' agreed Kylie, 'like—*When?*'

'Not recently! I was little.'

'How little?' She probed, '—like, a baby?'

'No—not a baby—I could walk and stuff, and do
things…'

'So you could talk then?'

'Yeah. Well, enough that I could know what I was
saying… what I was doing,' she added.

Katie's face had been inching unconsciously closer.
Leah's eyes kept flicking to the cluster of lashes
she'd neglected to blacken. But if Katie noticed her
staring, it was clear she didn't care.

'Woah,' she uttered. Then shifting even nearer,
hissed, 'So, was it, like, a big one?'

'No.'

She must be careful how she played it.

'…and was it like… hard?—I mean, *obviously* it was
hard—like difficult, to *do,* but I've always wondered
about afterwards…?'

Leah thought about it.

'Yeah. I guess so. A little.'

Katie sat back, reflecting. But when her thoughts finally settled, shrieked;

'But I would never have thought that *you*…!'

'Me neither!' added Kylie.

'Well, it's not like it's something I shout about.'

The four girls glanced at the shutters, the red light still flickering like a sleep-deprived eye lid, unseeing but daring them to test its alertness.

'No, of course, but you'd think there'd be signs or something, wouldn't you?'

'How do you mean?' But Leah understood; the years she'd spent terrified her crime like a cancer might appear on her skin.

'Well—sort of ways of knowing, of telling, if someone's a…you know…'

'…'

'…a Liar.' Samantha's voice cut through the lull like a fire cracker. If they'd forgotten she was there, they'd pay for the error.

'A Liar' she repeated. 'Like me?'

Katie was mute.

This time, it was Kylie who broke the silence.

'No—o. No. I didn't mean it like that! We don't mean that we've always thought you that you were…one— but it's just when *you* asked it, Sam, like, I wasn't… surprised? Maybe like I'd already guessed that you… had. Not that you're anything else bad, or anything. It's just—like, you're confident and stuff…?'

Katie was nodding earnestly, 'I've heard you need to be really confident to do it right.'

'Yeah, exactly,' said Kylie, 'And you're never shy or anything.'

The three of them turned towards Leah, who recoiled instinctively at the attention. She hated that none of them needed to voice what even she had been wondering. She tried to answer anyway.

'Well, it wasn't really a question of *how,* at the time. I just kind of... did. I had to.'

Katie sprayed a mouthful of foam across the circle. '*Had to*?' she shrieked. 'What does *that* mean?'

'It's strange to explain.'

'*Why*? You can tell us.'

'You can,' nodded Kylie, encouraging. She shifted a hand towards Leah's knee but then, hovering for a moment, seized a bottle cap instead. She passed it between her fingers. Circling the inside with her thumbnail, she scratched the soft plastic, waiting. Leah could see they were itching to know, but knew they wouldn't rush her. They were afraid to find out; Leah felt a tiny flush of pride.

But knowing from experience that it was too good to last, began slowly.

'It's just that I...'

'She's not going to tell us,' snapped Samantha. 'She never does.' It was more of a command than a prediction. The violence in her words made the other three jerk; Kylie dropped the bottle cap and scram-bled to retrieve it, as though a child caught with something she knew she shouldn't have. She plucked it from besides Katie's foot, where it landed, and the girls' eyes followed it into her palm. They stared, unseeing as she pressed the ridged metal lightly into her skin to make an imprint. No one dared look Samantha in the face.

'Anyway, she's told us already. She was little and

just said that she'd done something she hadn't.
Don't both shit your pants; that's barely even one.'

Katie and Kylie stayed silenced. But Leah, for
once, couldn't make herself stop.

'No. That wasn't it.' She said calmly. 'It was
something I did that I said I *didn't* do. But I did it,'
she added.

Furious at being undermined twice in one
evening, Samantha snatched the wine from Leah's
lap and glugged clumsily, staring cross-eyed at
the liquid as it vanished. When she'd finished she
slammed the glass down again, defiantly. A stray
bead of wetness spotted her chin.

'Whose turn is it?'

No one offered. Samantha wiped her lips dry
on her the back of her wrist, flashing her letters.
They were confidently grey against the cream
of her skin.

'Okay then, I'll go again,' she spat. 'Have-you-
everr... What's the worst thing you've ever done?'

She glared around the circle, lingering on Katie,
daring her to point out the breach in the rules.

She rounded on Kylie. 'If you're too good to Lie,
then second best—the worst thing you've done?'
she repeated.

Kylie's breathing dropped lower.

'Fine,' snapped Samantha. 'Well there's no point
asking *her*. *She's* already told us,' she flicked a hand
towards Leah. 'Go on then, Leah, say it—say
the word. What's the worst thing you've ever done?'

'I once told a Lie,' Leah breathed softly,
'a lie about killing my brother.'

Lucy Hamilton

Schrodinger's kitten

He checked the dashboard calendar: 1st June. He had said White Rabbits twice since it happened. Two months. But he still kept track; it would have been his weekend to have Tom. They'd be dragging their wakeboards from the river right now, or else, detaching cheese fries from a chilli bomb in Jerry's. Extra jalapeños; Tom's favourite. He still couldn't look at those slippery demons without being reminded of his son's olive irises; the exact same shade of green. Things had a way of lingering.

Since the accident, Steve had had trouble remembering. And there were things he kept forgetting to forget. Like his feelings for Shelly. They had ended on good terms, Tom had only been three at the time; deciding that staying together only ever pushed partnerships further apart. It was Newton's Third Law, or something like that. For every action there must be a reaction, both equal and opposite, so he had heard. At least her reactions were certainly the opposite. Shelly would keep the house, her dignity and Tom. Steve had kept the Citroen.

He glanced at the dashboard again; he had always had a head for dates. 1 June. The first of June. It taunted him like a face-down playing card. Clicking on the indicator, he thumbed its frayed edges. 1 June... Katie's birthday. The indicator snapped back. Weird really, that he'd remember his ex-wife's daughter's birthday when he forgot so many things of his own. It was like his memory had been replaced by hers.

He dropped down into second as he passed and
hoped she wasn't in the lounge to see him glance
up at the window. With the glare from the sun,
it was impossible to tell. Her Honda, a paradise blue,
was parked at an angle in the driveway. Odd that
she'd be home on a Saturday morning; he could
have sworn she had started back at work last week.
Maybe she'd just taken a holiday, to throw Katie
a party; that made sense.

Or perhaps her rota had changed. She might have
dropped weekend shifts altogether; understand-
able given everything. In fact, he had been amazed
at her wanting to start back so soon. Shelly's job
was emotionally draining. But maybe that was just
her way of coping; tangling herself in the insanity
of others. Whatever the reason, she was doing
amazingly. Her stitch-picker mind was still so sharp.

Steve's, on the other hand, was unravelling at
the seams. It was likely she had told him about
the change in her schedule and he had just forgotten. Yes—the more he thought about it, the
more he found himself remembering that Shelly
had said something like that the last time they'd
touched base. The distractions couldn't have
helped his memory: the damp vanilla of her hair;
the jingle of those earrings with the squiggles
he'd bought her and the fire he had almost caused
in her house.

'Your toast!' She had yelled from the kitchen.
'Steve!' A sharp intake of breath. The harsh sourness
still lingered in his throat. He coughed. 'If you're
trying to burn the house down, Steve, you could at
least warn me about it.' That sarcasm; it was almost
worth losing his mind just to hear.

He glanced back at the house in his rear-view mirror, cringing at the memory. To help himself to Shelly's food, Shelly's kitchen, was one thing; but to sit there in ignorance while the house filled with smoke. Four slices too! And he hadn't even been hungry. As if that was the weird part.

He had stood there, sheepishly in the doorway, muttering apologies as Shelly bounced the lever. Burning her fingers, she flicked charred multi-grain from the toaster and onto the sideboard. Her obstinacy was manic, but he suspected it was more of a reason not to have to look at him. She said nothing as she scooped the blackened crumbs into a pile. Four silent strides to the bin, Steve's lunacy cupped in her hands.

Dropping them in, she opened her palms and stared at the evidence lingering in the creases. Dusting them off, she tried twice to speak. She was struggling with something.

'You had no idea you'd put that on, hey?' she said, finally, softly, to the floor.

He shook his head twice. And though her back was still turned, she guessed at his answer and nodded. 'Steve, you don't live here anymore.' A silence, and he nodded. He knew that.

But Steve hadn't been able to make that knowledge stick. Since then, things had spiralled. It was becoming a regular occurrence, his going over there, uninvited, making Shelly's home theirs again. Not intentionally, of course, he would never assume to impose where he wasn't wanted. It's just that, in all honesty, he felt that he was. Before each visit, he could have sworn she had called him and hinted that she'd appreciate the company. More than hinted.

Katie's dad had been away from the house more and more. Working. Steve had no real reason to doubt Niall's honesty, he just hated to think of her alone in that house. She had Katie now, true, but she was still little. And since Tom... It must have been lonely. But obviously Steve was projecting.

Either way, that was what had made him think to buy her the kitten. She had always talked about getting one when they were still married. He had never liked them, ripping up the carpet when you forgot to let them out and always strutting around, knowing something he didn't. Then again, these days it seemed everyone did. But of course, Newton's law—she loved them.

She had one as a child. 'Nelson,' they had called him. And even when he had turned out to be a she, her parents had pronounced it terribly prudish to conform to gender specificity in felines.

That last bit had cracked him up. He had considered the detail such an insight into a childhood she rarely talked about. She was finally opening up to him, finally letting him inside, the sign he had needed to get down on one knee. He might forget his own name, but he would never forget that weekend in the lakes. That cottage with the drip, the way she had curved her hand to her mouth when he laughed at her story. And so it came as such a blow when he discovered he'd made it all up.

She had stood there in silence, gawping at him, eyes flitting from his face to the basketed kitten. And when he'd finished recalling her anecdote, a mutual shuffling had followed. And unsure whether to laugh, like she didn't get the joke, awaiting explanation, her smile had slowly faded. When his

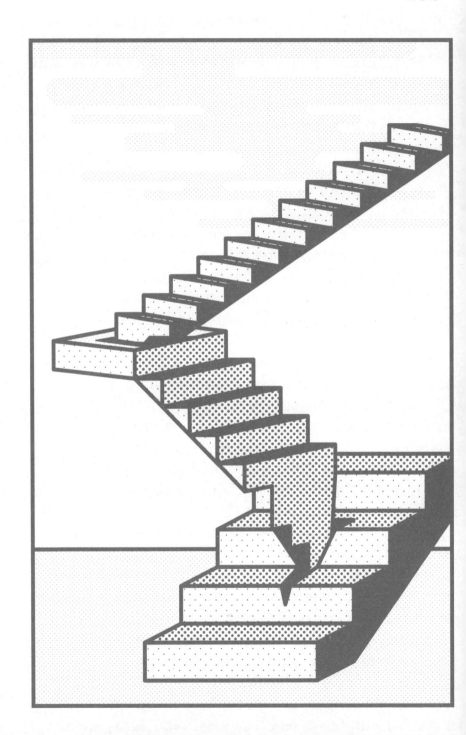

own offered none, her embarrassment had morphed into fear. And then anger.

What was he trying to do? Get back in by claiming to know more about her childhood than she did? Wouldn't she have remembered something like, erm... having a cat? Did he think she was an idiot?

No, he had said. *She wasn't an idiot.*

Of course she'd have remembered. Steve must have dreamed it. But the name thing had seemed so real. Maybe he had seen it on TV. He really was losing it.

She had thanked him for the kitten when he eventually succeeded in jostling it into her arms. Retreating back into the kitchen, she had held it at arm's-length, as though concerned its randomness was infectious. There really was no reason for Steve to have bought it. But here it was.

Steve had driven home to sleep off the weirdness, praying he might not dream up more cat tales of yore.

He had really pissed her off that time. Which is why he'd been surprised to see her photo flash up on his phone hours later; the cat wasn't looking so good. It was doing this thing with its hind leg. The left... Did it matter which bloody leg? He supposed no, not really. Steve would have to take it to the vet.

She had emerged with the basket and, strapping it into the Citroen's back seat, even pleasantly smiled, the story mix-up seemed almost forgotten. He supposed it was a good thing that she was a family psychiatrist. He guessed it made her more understanding. Overtly, at least; he hated to imagine the relief she must feel that he was no longer her problem.

At least, he shouldn't have been. Just two days ago, she'd come downstairs on her day-off to find him watching Rugby on Niall's widescreen, with one of

Niall's beers, half-empty, in his hand. There was canned macaroni bubbling away on the stove. The tin, partially opened, standing upright in the pan, the gas switched on full.

Shelly had been napping upstairs and smelled burning; a plasticky smell that he had smelled too, but had assumed it was her cooking something for their lunch. He hadn't liked to suggest that her culinary skills hadn't improved much. She hadn't found it that funny.

'You're getting worse, Steve.' He knew that he must be.

And soon the truth would have to come out about what had happened on the way to the vets. 'Happened'—like he hadn't let it. Like he wasn't responsible for everything wrong in her life. He'd avoided the topic, with the macaroni distraction, but the cat had been 'at the flat' for four days now. He was surprised she hadn't already started asking. Then again, perhaps she *had* asked and he just hadn't remembered. Perhaps he had already told her. But, that couldn't be right. There was no way she'd still be speaking to him.

He had retraced several hypothetical journeys, but found nothing. He just couldn't think why or where he might have stopped. A gas station, maybe; checks basket, cat jumps out. But this scenario didn't seem likely, his tank was still nearly empty. Or perhaps it really was at his flat. He could have gone back there on the way to grab his wallet— sensing freedom, the cat splits, like a Looney Tunes sketch... and then somehow replaces the clasp. He waited for a gap in the traffic and swung left. He would scour the park one more time.

His phone pulsed on the passenger seat. He glanced down.

Call me Steve. Far enough now.

His heart began to hammer. She was onto him.

He re-read the message several times until the screen dulled then went black.

At the lights, he jabbed the circle, and tapped in his pin.

Call me Steve. Far enough now.

He pressed reply.

Cat's fine Shelly. He held down backspace.

Do you want me to bring him round tonight? Too obvious.

He returned to the home-screen, dropped the phone in his lap and accelerated.

He'd call her later and confess, if he had to, if he hadn't solved the mystery by then.

His phone buzzed again.

Steve. Where the fuck are you?

He flung it back down and pulled a U-turn, ignoring the signs and the horns.

*

He pulled up on the street opposite her house, where a wide, open doorway framed her figure, like a tongue in a shout. She was fuming. He could see in the passenger mirror. He hesitated before stepping out onto the kerb.

She was already pacing in the driveway. Approaching, he went to say 'Shelly,' but his uvula choked him, and he swallowed her name. His arms reached towards her and she mirrored his gesture, but hers displayed fury. She side-stepped his concern.

She was circling like a shark in one of Tom's cartoons. He had not seen her this way for a long time. Her ponytail was unwashed and lopsided, sliding out of a hairband stretched loose at the staple. The hood of her sweater was turned inside out; and the label stuck up from the neck. Every time she turned her back, his eyes were drawn towards it.

A small, flat face appeared behind Shelly in the crack of the doorway. 'Happy Birthday, Katie!' He remembered.

Katie's face smiled back for just a second, like she had forgotten to be sad. But then disappeared back inside. As she turned, for just a moment, he thought he saw the tip of a tail flick up from her folded arms. *I did, I did saw a…*

'Who the fuck is Katie, Steven?' Shelly spat through gritted teeth.

He frowned, puzzling out what she might mean and then… 'Oh right, hah, yeah, sorry, it's not "Katie," is it?'

But he couldn't for the life of him think what else it might be. Maybe she liked *Kate,* now, or *Katherine.*

Shelly had stopped pacing and was glaring at him.

'Where the hell have you been Steve?' She exhaled.

He thought for a second. Her question confused him. In his flat, then his car, searching for that bastard cat. But he kept this last part to himself. 'And don't even try, Steve. Don't say you forgot.' First, she'd have to tell him what it was he hadn't forgotten.

'It's Saturday, Steve!'
He knew that.

'Tom, Steven. Your son?'

But he hadn't forgotten about Thomas. How could he? He was in every thought. Every memory an agony. She couldn't really believe that he had. He stared at her, blankly, and her face seemed to melt.

'You were meant to pick him up at 11. I'm supposed to be at work, for Christ's sake!'

There was a silence. Her words filled his mouth, but he couldn't make himself spit them out.

'Shelly. That's not funny.'

She opened her eyes wide, in sorry disbelief.

He realised then that she hadn't been joking.

She seemed to deflate.

'Tom doesn't think it's very funny either.' She said, flatly. 'He's upstairs, and he's pretty cut up.' A pause, and then: 'Steve... You might want to say sorry.'

She surveyed his frozen features for a few moments longer, and then, shaking her head, turned back towards the house.

Her words stretched in contrails behind her. The smoke of their edges already blurring. Tom... was upstairs. That's what she had said.

A million questions flooded his mind.

Tom was dead.

He was dead. He knew he was dead. He could see it all again, tracing ghosts down the driveway. The flashing blue lights in the rain on the road, that eggshell matte paint, the smell of the waiting room, and the waiting. The damp jacket condensing the polythene bag, Lego figurine still clinging to the zipper. It was missing one hand. That damned bike and all those lost Saturdays.

He felt sick. He was going to be sick. He dropped into a crouch on the driveway. The pockmarks of pebbles swirled, making him dizzy. He fingered their brail but the meaning evaded him.

Denim pinched his skin as he lowered his knees to rest on the ground. He stayed there for several moments, forcing each breath, drowning in answers.

Every detail in his mind as real as the concrete. He pressed his forehead against its coolness.

Then tore it away, and forced himself onto his feet.

He lunged at the door. It swung inwards and resounded off the corner of the worktop.

He loitered on the precipice of the kitchen; and the edge of what he couldn't remember.

Then the ache overcame him.

He sprang from the doorway, tearing into the hallway and boots trailing a drumroll on the thick staircase carpet. He rounded the landing, and hammered pale panels.

Tom's bedroom was empty. He tried the play-room, still no one. And the bathroom. And rooms he had already checked. Doors to cupboards, flung open, swung limply on hinges, each bearing a hollow as real as the child they'd said goodbye to.

Finally, he collapsed onto his old quilted duvet, spilling sobs into the vacuum of his world. He reached his arms up and grasped Shelly's pillow, pulling it into his face. He breathed her in. Her wholesome vanilla, that granary bread of her breaths.

A gentle knock at the door and he froze.

A murmur. 'Steve?'

Pushing tears from his eyes with the balls of his hands, he sat upright. It was Katie.

They stared at each other, neither trusting their words.

Her head dipped a little as she stepped through the doorway, as though ducking beneath an invisible cordon. Her feet shuffled slowly through the dust of the carpet, and when she stopped by the bed he watched toes curl and uncurl inside scruffy socks.

He stared up into eyelashes damp as his own that clung to each other in a brackish embrace. She perched on the mattress beside him, staring down at the varnish of nibbled pink glitter. Her fingers were clammy and trembling.

'It's my mum.' She said, quietly. 'Shelly', she added for his benefit when he didn't seem to register. 'There's... She's... I think something's wrong.'

Her breaths mingled with his in the shrill static silence, that neither of them seemed ready to break. When someone finally did it was Steve, with a question.

But before she had answered he already knew.

'Well... like toast in the toaster.' said Katie. 'She keeps making it black, and she won't scrape all the badness away.'

Her voice began to crack.

'And this morning, when I'm five...' She raked in a sob.

'She said it isn't my birthday. But it is. I've remembered. Even you said it is! And... and then she kept calling me Tom.'

Her sobs became suddenly calm. And her earlobes pulsed crimson, her nail beds blinked back.

'But Tom's dead, Steve, isn't he? Tom died.'

Lucy Hamilton

Ragnarok

Day 911. Snowing again. The smell of burning on the wind.

Sleep slid off him like an oversized garment, leaving him bare. Awakening, all colour was drained from the world. That was his life now. Why was it always brighter in his dreams? Once, sleep had been a thing to fear. He had felt content knowing that life awaited the end of each slumber, a beacon of light which extinguished nightmares. *Is this life?* He wasn't sure any more. Life had been joy, life had been his son, life had been her.

His life was buried beneath the snow 334 days ago. *Two snow angels.* He rubbed the centre of his ring finger, still unaccustomed to the emptiness there. The ring itself was in his pocket, out of sight but scarcely out of mind.

Nightmares had taken over. He could not count the number of times which he had willed himself to awaken, to ascend from this hell. Nor could he count the refusals to do so. He had had enough of living day by day. Each day was the same. Only the numbers were different, the casualties.

That burning smell. *I must keep moving.*

Not even the snow was pure. Discoloured by the ashen earth. God's grief for his children, descending to their world in an attempt to conceal man-made scars. The attempt was futile. The snow was too sparse, even the tears of Gods insufficient for the purpose of masking mankind's sin. He should have cried more. Or was it shame that God felt?

Rising to his feet, he rolled up the ragged old blanket before fastening it to his back with the knots he had taught his son. He was Atlas, but the world had toppled from his shoulders to shatter into a million pieces at his feet. All he could do was stare at the broken fragments which remained of his former life. In a previous life, this would have been noon. The sun's light was a haze, a pupil smothered by a cataract of dull cloud. It was at once muted by the perpetual darkness of the skies, and blinding in its trivial glory when the man-made clouds deigned to disperse. But that was rare.

How must Earth look from space? It might well be indistinguishable from the darkness of the galaxy, a few stray wisps of smoke allowing some sunlight to peer out like a nosy neighbour looking through a curtain. *All of my neighbours are dead.* It was not uncommon to see others on the road, yet you had to be cautious. There were, after all, the ones who wished you harm, the ones who placed themselves at the top of the food chain. The others were hiding, or wandering like he was, trying to find a purpose. *Am I?*

He remembered the initial sound of the bombs, the explosions which brought down buildings and their builders alike, an involuntary exodus to a land beyond the veil. They pounded now at the walls of his memory, breaking through, an insurmountable mound of debris on the lines of his train of thought. As the cacophonous barrage faded, he became aware that he was kneeling, his head held in a brace position between his legs.

The Fourth World War was a memory, but that did not mean it was distant. *Some memories your mind refuses to let go.* He was back on the fields then, officers shouting through earpieces, the Behemoths firing their long cannons, the AA guns their skyborne missiles, the poor bastards on the ground their wide range of guns. *And then the comets, like strikes from Thor's hammer pummelling the earth into submission.* It was impossible now to tell whether all the chaos had been caused by the nukes or the comets, though they may well have fallen days apart.

The desolation had reduced him from a father, husband and soldier to a wondering wanderer, a traveller with no destination in this world. Family man to lone ranger. A crusader without a cause. Causes were something that he'd abandoned a long time ago.

Fire-blackened houses stood, skeletal, leaning lazily over towards what might have once been a road. He could only pray that this road could succeed where others had failed him. Dotted along the highway to hell were assorted vehicles, all of them abandoned. There were tanks with their cannons blown to pieces, cars missing wheels and wing-mirrors. Some of them even lacked seats; the occupants were strewn across the ground, robbed of chunks of flesh, eyes open in shocked horror. If they were still there.

A rusted wheel cover lay on the road before him. Lifting it up tentatively in his gloved hands, he raised it to the dim daylight, trying to create a golden glow. The sun did not comply. *Is this the best this place has to offer?* Moronic. He grimaced at his own naivety, tossed the un-golden plate to the ground with a soft thump as it plopped into the snow.

He walked past an unruly knot of black wire, twisted and warped, the ashen coat giving the impression of liquorice. His son hated liquorice. He took after his father like that.

Another tank. Sometimes the militia could be seen driving what remained of their vehicles; he supposed they must have underground bases dotted around the country, but the lesser troops such as he had been wouldn't know about that. The upper echelons in their overcoats and medals would be sworn to secrecy, mouths sealed by the promise that their families would be safe. *Sealed now by death.* For even Gods and presidents could lie to their flock...

As he trudged through the layer of ash, he tried not to think about what-or whom- they had once belonged to. Hands, twisted beyond belief, reached up out of the debris, as if to grasp the stars or plead to their God. God didn't answer. He never did. Enveloped in blissful ignorance, God had abandoned his children. *Or is it smug surveillance?*

He avoided the corpses, which with each breeze appeared less human. He had made some of them, not even counting his days in the military. His first was when a couple of them had threatened his son. Never would he have believed his inner brutality until that moment. The field was different. The assailant had been left on the ground, face a pulp which was indistinguishable from his body. It had been snowing then, too, but he had been no angel.

His second...

He rubbed his finger again, a habit which must have appeared stupid, yet was of even more importance to him now that he no longer wore his ring. It did not dull the pang of loss. He did not want that. Would not have it. He deserved to be haunted by it forever, compensation for his failure, a moral debt he could only try his best to repay. He was about to ask God again if there was anything more he could have done, but then remembered he didn't exist anymore. Was this how Lucifer felt when he was cast down? As he stood there, he found it hard to remember if there had ever been a paradise to lose.

A helicopter was to his left, having apparently collided with a house. The three rotary blades spun in the wind, struggling against nature's cascading white blanket. The cross they almost formed had no place in this new world. It reminded him of the church he attended until 332 days ago. The hymns would warm his heart, but nothing could warm him now. *Not even the fires.* He put his hand into the flames wreathed around the helicopter, watched his skin blacken like the rest of the world had. He imagined the flames dancing in her eyes as they sat around the fireplace at home. That hurts. He took his hand away.

He again rubbed his finger, the empty space which had formerly been filled by that circle of his life. *And what is left when life is taken away?* There were times when death seemed appealing, a welcome release. But most of the time, he felt like he was dead already. *I just got sent the wrong way.*

Tremors would still run through the earth, delivering desolation without discrimination. Just as tremors still ran through him now. A gentle push sent the door of the house to the ground, an ugly dust cloud belching up as particles of the door rose up before fluttering with false beauty back to their resting place, an imperfect impression of snow. *Snow.* Snow angels were unearthed as the snow in his memory melted from the heat of his emotions, eyes open wide, vivid with accusation. Closing his own eyes could not banish them. They were a burn-in imprinted on the backs of his eyelids. *Burn-in?* He could barely remember the last time he watched a television.

Well, he could remember the faces. The President deciding that it was time to release the nukes after a trivial disagreement, standing at the podium before the rest of the world via a television screen. The state senators and congressmen in the crowd, divided as ever, some of them sacrificing their opinion to spend more time on their pads. Many of them would probably have escaped the chaos, would be hidden in some presidential bunker somewhere, or would have used airships or Arks to retreat to someplace where they could live with their warped collective conscience for the rest of their days, as he would. *At least they can divide the responsibility.* He had no bunker, no refuge. *Not that shelter helps much anyway.* Whoever had lived here had discovered that fact well enough. The house looked like a bomb had... *Never mind.*

He stepped warily into the building, snow descending on him through the gaping wound in the decrepit roof. A left turn took him into the living room. *Television.* He pressed the remote control, and he was with his wife again, their newborn son.

Peppa Pig was oinking away on the screen, her family
laughing, just as they once had. The years went
by in a second. His son was seven, reading fairy tales
and myths and the Bible in the big armchair.
Then he was gone, along with his mother, the last
memories he had of them being cowering and
screaming as he failed to save them from the fallen
beings which once had been men…

The remote was aimed at god, but it went hrough
the shattered screen of the television, spewing out
its long-dead batteries as it broke to pieces against
a wall. He went for the stairs, wanting to believe that
they would take him up to heaven to see his angels.
*And as we wind on down the road, our shadows taller
than our soul…*

His soul had withered every day since their
absence, and shadows had engulfed him. And he
still couldn't find the woman buying a stairway
to heaven. If it was any consolation, his spirit was
always crying for leaving. But it wasn't. Each
step whispered like a futile prayer, and it did not
take too many unanswered pleas to the heavens
before he reached the top.

It was no utopia, no Olympus. Any god would
do, but he had heard those who said they were
all one and the same. There was no pearly gate. He
would have opened the door, had there been one
there; all that remained was a single hinge, like
a hand reaching out to grasp a non-existent reality.

The first bed was too hard, its mattress rotted
and torn by what looked like knife slashes. *Or bears.*

The next room had been similarly scavenged.
People were like that these days. They had to be, to
survive. *And to die.* This bed was too large for his

taste, too soft, too obviously empty. He left the room and entered a third.

A child's room. This bed was just right. There were no bears to give him a fright if he went to sleep; animals had been the first food source. They had to feast on dog at first, all the while concealing it from his son. He had never been a dog person, so that was easy. But what came after...

Hellboy watched him from his A3 prison on the wall, face possessed by a perpetual scowl. *This is his world.* It smelt like Hell too. *Like death.* He stepped over to the closet, opening the door. One glance was all he needed. He quickly left the room and found himself retching on the staircase. Slowly, he rose from the porridge-like puddle he had created. A messy painting. *Almost as messy as this world.* Wiping the splashback of liquid disgust from his face with a grotty old sleeve, his thoughts returned to his angels, what he would have done— had done—to men who did such things to them.

He remembered the man who was eating *their* flesh. 'It's d-d-dog,' he whimpered, 'Y-y-you can have it.' *It wasn't dog.* The zombie had kept talking. 'Y-y-you can have it if y-y-you want. Y-y-you and y-your family.' A gunshot had ended the thing's moaning.

Back downstairs, he opened the kitchen drawers and cupboards—those which were still left. Most of the doors had been taken, perhaps to use as pillows, perhaps to use as shields, perhaps just because they could be. *Canned oysters.* He rotated the can in his hand, lifted the slightly-open lid. A rancid stench hit his nostrils like a nuke. *The world is your oyster.* His father used to tell him that. He continued turning the can in his hand, tried to decide whether his father knew him from God and an oyster from an ashtray.

Time to leave. There was nothing more for him here. He stepped over the face-down door and back onto the road. Evening. The sky's blindness had intensified, yet the snow still fell. *Snow angels.* He rubbed his finger again as he watched the snow form another shroud for his dead. *Death.* It kept returning to his mind. The fact that he lived when so many others had died made it feel as if he had cheated fate, and was standing back at death's door, unsure of whether to knock.

Voices tore through his thoughts.

'Stop right there!' Two figures stood a little further down the former road, one of them clutching a gun. The other held what appeared to be a baseball bat studded with nails.

'Are you ready to meet your fucking maker?' said Thing One.

He was. He had a few things to say to his maker. He patted the pistol by his side.

The two Things were advancing on him. He drew the pistol, held it firmly before his person as a warning. Said not a word.

'Put the gun down, or we'll blow your fucking brains out.' Thing One again. Thing Two was rather quiet. The pistol stayed where it was.

'Are you fucking deaf?'

He fucking wasn't. But he didn't fucking move. He stared at the snow on the ground intently.

Another explosion went through his mind. He saw white. And then, at last, he heard the angels.

Samuel Wadkin

Fiction

It's empowering to know what I do. Isn't it absurd
how little nuggets of information can change
where you'll end up living. If you can call prison
'living'. I don't know if you can. But then again,
I wouldn't actually know about that. I always smile
when I think this. Not that I am not aware of
the perceived 'horror' of prison life, but I imagine
the situation would work in my favour, if I was
to end up there. You may see this as arrogance, but
I suppose you are entitled to your opinion.

And by saying this, it does not mean to say that
I do not care about anyone's opinion, in fact the

reverse is true. But the identity of the opinion holder is all that matters. And yours does not. Shame really, because I would actually quite like to tell you how it came to be that I am sitting here, basking in the embers of my own mischievousness. Maybe that is the wrong lexical choice. Or maybe it isn't. The 'severity' of a person's actions is entirely subjective. What may be deemed utterly unacceptable in one city, may be renowned as permissible in another. So the consequences of our actions are entirely dependent on our location.

It isn't like I am a person that cannot be weighed down and sunk... like the hope of a downtrodden child pining for approval from a distant parent. But it is not, as is the case for most people, guilt that weighs me down. I think, and you may agree, that guilt is an abstract concept anyway. I think you'd be intrigued to hear about how I've perused away my hours, where I've been. And where she is, or was, or will be. I'm not going to give anything away just yet, even the choice of tense I use to detail another character can give away the plot. Emphasis on character because the narration of fiction always includes this word. What intrigues me, perhaps not you as you won't have considered this, is how there is always a generic assumption present—that characters remain fictitious. Whoever concluded that the tantalising hints a narrative slips in are anything but what has actually been experienced? Who surmised that the perfect crime cannot be hidden behind a collection of adverbs?

Maria Vegro

Chase

It was a picturesque blue day in June, where Hugh could be found. He was perched high up in a leafy oak tree. Rabid dogs tore around the base of the trunk, spitting and snarling. A breath of short exasperation puffed out into the air. The men who had trod behind these beasts were far off in the distance, pin pricks to the squinted eye.

Apart from stealing one fleeting glimpse of these four stony faces, Hugh had never set eyes on his pursuers before. After whipping around, his chest now heaved deeply from his unexpected sprint. The three canines lurched around his feet, saliva flicking from their open jaws. The men clearly had not vouched to running. They had trodden, slowly, not a panic-stricken leap through the air as Hugh's had been but a calculated clop of feet, moving in time with each other.

Hugh scanned the ground below him. His heart raced like a hummingbird's and tension oozed through his muscles. The clock on his wrist showed 4:4. A thin wavy crack ran through the last digit. He swore aloud. A new birthday present, already marked. He examined the other trees that grew close to him, his eyes lingering on a nearby target that was almost at his height. The one supporting him was barren of twigs, and the only object that could be thrown was clamped on his wrist with a crack down its face. He wobbled slightly, a breeze toppling his balance. Aiming straight on, the watch was released from its owner and launched through the air. A split second's distraction caught

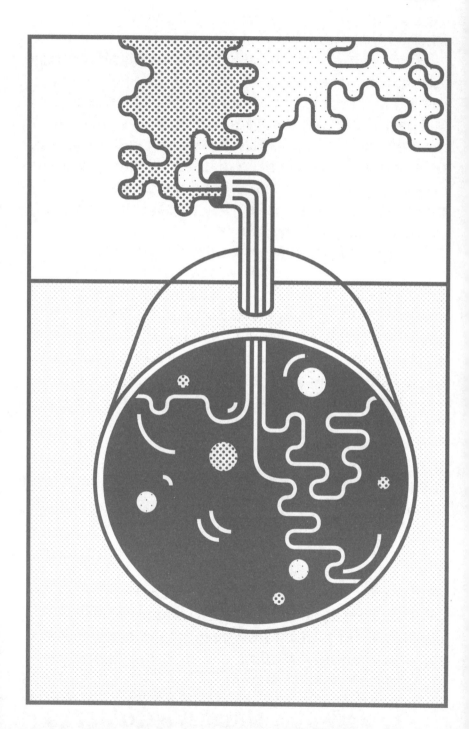

the eyes of the crazed canines, the swivelling digits reached their target and shattered.

Hugh's stomach fell, twice as far as he did. Pelting through the trees, twigs slapped his cheeks, blood speckling a trail behind him. His pursuers raced in a battle with his pounding pulse. Barks snapped through the air, and ruffled leaves blocked his vision, as if outraged to have been disturbed. The stamina Hugh had built up over the previous months surged through his calves, they dug into the ground below him and sprung him on.

Dozens of trees flew past him, whilst the dogs' cries grew quieter. He turned back and double took as a singeing pain seized his leg and forced him nearly to a halt. Pain welling up in his eyes, he hopped once, twice, fell. His attackers leapt mercilessly onto his torso when a sharp whistle pierced the wooded silence. Scanning the trees desperately, Hugh found no one in sight. His legs sprang him to polarity and he began again a restless sprint of fear.

It was with surprise that he found himself recognising houses and he realised he was now on the outskirts of his crescent street. It followed a curve round past his neighbours, past a lone cyclist pedalling slowly through the sunshine.

Relief flooded his chest as his front door presented itself. Giving himself a chance to finally breathe, he slowed as he came within its reach. Condensation steamed the metallic handle, his clammy hands slipping to let himself in. The door swung back and what was behind it could never have been anticipated in all Hugh's wildest dreams.

Maria Vegro

Vices

If you live, are you really alive? What classifies you
into the perceived superiority of being a living
human being? Is it the constant seeping of red liquid
through your arteries, that slips your mind? Is it
your heart sprinting at a thousand beats per minute,
the soar of stimulants, the only substances that
can supply satisfactory speed? What is 'should' and
who decides it?

Is it reaching that ecstatic infinite pleasure, when
your body is linked to someone you think you love?
You, thinking you know what love is. Giving and
taking become visible verbs.

Is it the employment of your patience and anxiety
in restriction that gives you potency, a hazy sense
of control driving your brain to correlate emptiness
with good or bad? Or is it charging, restrained,
eyes barely open but barely closed? Hunger gnaws

out a hole in your stomach and your brain when it is voluntary.

Is it licking the last remnants of a double, extra special Gordon's measure of regret from around your mouth? Is it staring deep into the soul of your own personal convert to heliology, or is it the tie of forbidden truths not untold, latching the secret keepers close in the presence of the subject? It is always a good idea to have another drink.

Is it a warm haze of intoxication fuzzing over your 'better' judgement? Or is it your better judgement being reversed in the presence of an idolised confederate. Is it the joy in your offspring's eyes, as they tear light-reflecting paper away from their source of momentary entertainment? Only a child portrays greed in such a way, emanating content in the eyes of their audience.

Is it the tranquillity than only isolation seems to bring, a lack of words sounding your voice? Is it the withdrawal into the smallest shell of yourself that I have never set eyes on? Is it the outburst of precipitation from the heavens, soaking you in drips of pathetic fallacy? Or is it the warmth of a thousand tropical sunbursts?

I think it is a tongue enveloping itself in steaming bitter liquid, a cardboard cup full of generosity. It is the embrace of a companion at the coldest point of another's life. It is the upturned mouth created when a grey fog stretched out across all that was visible, and all that was invisible. We never speak about death; it is the inevitable taboo governing our consciousness at all miniscule minutes and hours.

Maria Vegro

Manchester

The many legged spider had caught his prey. The
two flies were walking into his web, tequila clouds
swirling through their judgement and presenting
the home of the predator as an abode of appeal. They
had known something was amiss as they travelled
with the spider, humour and shared smoke disguising
him as a friend. Sitting atop the spider's lap, one
of the flies, B, had felt a worry crawling into its brain
and, squinting outside, none of the surroundings
could be recognised. The second fly, A, exuberated
ease, a lukewarm cigarette lit to its mouth. They

couldn't remember leaving where they had been but they acknowledged entering the arachnid's lair.

Grimy grey walls stood sheer and proud above. Stained wooden boards covered the floor, with a few hinting at a history of laminate. The flies followed their host's direction slowly up the staircase, swaying legs reaching out with hesitation for the next step. A turn of a key behind them heightened the foreboding that had wrapped around their intestines. B swivelled its head in an attempt to search for something but was intercepted by a gleaning grin from the spider. They couldn't remember his, or was it her, name.

The silent party reached a standstill. The two flies met each other's eyes and wide eyed looks of surprise were exchanged. A puzzling scent wafted through the room, one of everything just being not quite right. Adrenaline surged through the spider. He turned towards the flies and with a smile that didn't meet his many eyes, beckoned his prey closer. Entertainment was promised. An attempt at a reassuring tone was made to convince the flies that they had made the right decision by coming here. An invitation to the room where he collected his trophies swarmed the consciousness of the flies. A nodded in agreement, the last three Jaeger-bombs blocking out any sense of sense. A flicker of sobriety flooded across B, who remained motionless, stubborn feet stood stationary.

The spider skulked opposite from them now, his manic eyes flitting from prey to prey. They registered hesitation from its right-hand side. A scatter of skeletal legs prepared themselves to launch forward before a hollow laugh echoed through the lightless space. B was smiling, willing the spider to stop, to reconsider. Its eyes told a tale of agreement, that the two would concede to accept his invitation.

The spider scrambled eagerly across the floorboards, his legs scratching softly through the silence. Just before reaching out for the door handle, he turned and eyed the flies greedily. His gaze lingered on their thighs.

Frantically, without time to think, B blurted out a hurried request to smoke one more cigarette in the peace of the street. The spider smirked and reassured the two of how welcome they were to smoke in his trophy room. The tone of authority in his voice was poorly concealed. He watched his prey for a moment longer but, convinced of his own control, he turned to face the door once more.

In a surge of speed, B seized A and made for the staircase. With a flash, A snapped back to sense and followed suit. The two flies streamed drunkenly down the stony steps, derelict walls towering over them. The key was jammed into the lock on the spider's front door and B struggled to open it, screaming with frustration.

Finally, fresh air flooded through the flies as A wrenched the door open and launched the key into the night, the house hiding under cloud's shadows. The sound of a spider's many feet rushing down the stairs writhed through the silence but to no avail.

The spider stopped abruptly, his nose breathing in the fresh scent of food. As he peered into the darkness, he saw the two flies banging on the doors of a bus before they snapped open and allowed entry. His prey had escaped.

Maria Vegro

Spring Heeled Jack

He can spring like a goat,
He can jump like a cat,
He comes at night,
He's robed in white,
He appears in a flash,
He disappears in a dash.

Pip stood at the bottom of Park Hill. He had been told
to bring a stick for the night's event; a stick he
brought. It held firm in his hand just as a bat would.
He was ready. Pip put one work-booted foot in
front of the other, and started to charge up the hill.
Determination crinkled across his face, anger
exploding through his heart. Too long had they been
afraid of the man that roamed Park Hill through
the shadow of night. His knuckles had gone white,
the wood began to splinter. Sweat soared from
his head, tingled in his armpits and dropped from his
chin droplet by droplet, landing on the chest of
his ripped faded overalls. Adrenaline coursed through
him like a charge of electricity. His boots continued
to trudge. He stopped. He had found the edge.
Men were rooted around the sandy brick monument,
stale sweat creeping through the air. Expressions
were haunted as the night wrapped around them like
a cool unstable blanket, too tight to burst through,
too loose for security. The monument stood tall
before Pip; he knew what it stood for but to him it
was a beacon of a different message. To him it wasn't
a monument—it was a warning. A warning of the
one who could jump so high—the one who could
scare you half to death—the one who disappeared—

the one beyond the grasp of any man—the one they named Spring Heeled Jack. Tonight was Pip's first time. He stood on the edge, thousands of men before him. Pip could feel it in his marrow; tonight was the night the men of Sheffield would catch Spring Heeled Jack. Pip was alert, and while his bones felt ready to shake, he was determined. He stood firm. Shoulder to shoulder with the men beside him like a brick wall; nothing could get through their mortar. Getting through wasn't the problem though; the mass of sky above was. How high could he really jump?

Don't go out at night, he'll come for you,
Don't forget your stick, he'll come for you,
Don't go misbehaving, he'll come for you,
Don't forget your wits, he'll come for you.

'Ey, lad, this tha first time?' a gruff looking man said, thudding Pip on the shoulder. His hands were black, his skin stained with the city's labour. In a few years Pip knew he would look the same. He cast his eyes over the men; they were all at various stages of deterioration. Backs hunched, fingers lost, eyes squinting, hands scarred, bodies worn, marked by a lifetime of work. These men held their stories in their skin: they were broken, battered and bruised beyond repair, yet they would not falter, they would not sway. These men before Pip, these men were made of steel.

'Eh did tha 'ere me lad?' Pip was brought back to focus on the man next to him.

'Ye, but am ready. Av 'eard all the stories,' Pip replied confidently, his knuckles turning whiter by the second.

'Ar re'me'be wen it wo jus' two of us flinging es sticks ab'at, nah look thes thou'ands,' the man went on, swirling his stick above his head.

He was right, the rumour of the vigilante had spread like wild fire through the city streets. The population was on the verge of mass hysteria. People double locked their doors at night. When the sun faded from the sky, curtains were drawn, people huddled together in their rooms barely daring to breathe.

> He can spring like a goat,
> He can jump like a cat,
> He comes at night,
> He's robed in white,
> He appears in a flash,
> He disappears in a dash.

'Yeh look frightened kid, yeh sure yeh al reyt?' The man looked down at Pip, his eyes piercing through him like a man who had seen the world's troubles. Like a man who saw life for what it was: a struggle.

Pip looked firmly at him. 'Am fine,' he said, his tone angry.

The man gave a grunt before he returned to staring ahead into the vast throng of men. Pip copied, but as he did an odd feeling began to stir inside him. One that caused his eyes to twitch, his lips to quiver, his hands to tremble. Pip willed his body to stop; it wouldn't. He looked up at the man trying to conceal the emotions of his face beneath his tattered flat cap. The man whipped his eyes to look at Pip in his peripheral. Pip avoided eye contact and looked

straight ahead. The man continued to stare. Pip felt
his gaze blister on his face, causing Pip to rotate
himself to meet the man's eyes.

'Wot is it kid?' the man said gruffly, yet there was
an air of softness to his voice as he rubbed the tired
from his eyes.

'Wot de yeh do?' Pip asked, a slight tremble to
his voice.

'With wot?' The man looked up to the sky,
searching for something he was sure he would find.
Eventually.

'When he comes, wot do I do?'

'Ah ryt, why din't yeh se that in the first place',
the man said with a chuckle running through
his face. 'Wot tha need t'do is as soon as tha sees
him, 'nd tha will see him, tha need t'raise the
stick high 'nd charge him.'

'Charge?'

'Yeh, charge, as fast as tha can, cos he's a slippery
lil devil 'nd he can disappear or jump out of thos
gaps before tha knows it.'

'Av you eve caught him?' Pip asked.

'Well, no,' the man replied with resistance in
his voice.

Pip hesitated, and then asked 'As anyone ever
caught 'im?'

'Well...No...But that's not the point...' The man
opened his mouth to offer further explanation,
but thought better of it after seeing Pip's whimpering
face. He was just a lad after all. 'Nah quit yeh askin'
'nd stand up straight.'

Pip did as he was told, though he began to wonder
what the point of all this was. Thousands of strong
men stood, waiting with their sticks for a figure that

may or may not appear, a figure that, as was
becoming clear to Pip, they could not catch. Why?

Moments had passed. The quiver had stopped
but his morale had slumped, in fact Pip just wanted
to sit down or go home. But that was weakness
to be ridiculed among them, so he kept in formation
and waited. A pulsation filtered through the crowd.
A light began to shine through the cracks in the
men's arms. *He's here,* Pip thought to himself, *he's
actually here.* He started to patter on his tip toes,
ready to sprint, holding the stick higher. Pip looked
to his side and saw the man grasping the stick at
the other end. He wasn't looking at Pip, though.
He was looking out towards the bright shining light.

'Nah wot 'av we told you lot ab'at this,' a voice
rippled through the crowd, firm, a whisper of authority within. 'Nah clear off and stop the nonsense.'

'No,' another shouted. 'His real en we're gunna
stay 'ere until we catch him.'

'Not if I've anything to se about it,' the voice from
before grumbled.

Men started to be pulled from the crowd and
thrown down the hill like they were disposable.
That's when Pip saw them storming through in their
pressed navy uniforms, the silver buttons glinting
in the moonlight, their hats giving them the height
of authority. Pip bowed his head, trying to shield
himself from the light. The light suddenly flickered
and went out. Pip opened his eyes, and as he looked
up he saw a hailstorm of stones soaring over him.
He heard expletives being uttered between ignored
orders. The policemen cowered, trying to deflect
the bits of rubble and various stones that were flying
their way.

'Eh'I'se—clear off—'nd n'bdy—il get hurt,' a police-man dictated between shielding his face from oncoming stones. Pip looked around him and saw that the men of Yorkshire paid no heed to police threats such as this. Instead of retreating, they began to clang their sticks together. Pip felt the energy of the men as they smashed their sticks so hard they splintered with every bang. Pip felt geared up with momentum as he presented his stick as high as he could, ready for it to be clanged. He closed his eyes in anticipation, a smile stretched across his face. Nothing happened. A silent pause beamed around the park. It was only for a moment before a rapture of noise hit every surface. Pip opened his eyes to see the men attacking forward, charging in the direction of the policemen.

'Oh,' Pip said to himself, lowering his stick. 'Well I guess that's that then.' He dropped his stick and sprinted with all the speed he could muster to join the chaotic crowd.

He swung himself in, all singing and dancing. Pip threw a kick this way and that, throwing a few punches, too. He felt exhilarated by it all, even if his blows kept meeting air more than they did the opposition. He was a part of it. After a few minutes, Pip began to realise he had no idea who he was fighting with. Was it the steel men of Sheffield, the ones who work till their backs ache, or was it the policeman? He had no clue. He was just happy to be involved in whatever this was. Through Pip's elation sirens could be heard, lots of them. The noise pierced through the commotion like a needle through cotton. All the men went silent. The policemen stood up from the ground, grabbing their batons where they could, their arms folded, their stance strong as more police began to pour out of cars. They lined up shoulder to shoulder, a thick strong line in front of the rough haggard men. Pip could feel the anticipation swelling around the park. Pip knew it was the calm before the storm. There was going to be a fight and it was going to be a good one. Or so he thought.

Pip readied himself to join the fight. He placed his feet apart one in front of the other and put his fists up, one slightly higher than the other. Just as his Dad had taught him. Before he knew it, the men were running full pelt, but not in the direction Pip had expected. They weren't running towards the policemen, they were running down the hill. Pip chased to catch up with them, and as he did he saw the man he had been talking to before. The one who had been telling him about Spring Heeled Jack.

'Ey, lad, 'ow's it going?' he shouted through the stampede, his voice nearly lost. Pip gave him a nod. He wasn't sure if he could run and talk.

'Yeh had fun?' he asked. Pip nodded again. 'G'd, I'll si tha next time then.' Pip looked at the man as he realised what his words meant. Pip, unsure what to do now, nodded again and continued to run down the hill.

He can spring like a goat,
He can jump like a cat,
He comes at night,
He's robed in white,
He appears in a flash,
He disappears in a dash.

Emily Elizabeth France

Fade

We were expecting a war, grand and all consuming; had pre-emptively titled it to follow two others that were named already, claiming seven countries' conflict to represent the globe in a century of comparative peace. Three made sense, inevitable and deserved for crimes too long unatoned for: crimes against a world perceived to be spinning out of control, against a god, against ourselves; crimes of action and inaction, surely guaranteeing retribution, divine or otherwise. But there was no great war; nothing grand and exciting and apocalyptic. We did not utterly destroy the planet, just altered it beyond our ability to reverse. We did not destroy ourselves, just gradually slid into this. Cold, grey and without malice or compassion.

Scholars and scientists thought apathy would be our downfall, that surely our wilful ignorance spelt disaster. But we saved ourselves at the last possible moment, when necessity demanded. And we haven't paid, not really. We have an infuriating knack for self-preservation. Selfish and lacking any shred of foresight, but somehow always adequate. When our world began to change, there was no mighty battle for resources. Yes, there were a few skirmishes at the beginning. But at some point, we remembered that war itself is taxing. Trading blandly when convenient and otherwise retreating into our own small communities, we endured.

No one thought world peace would look like this, but peaceful we are. The population dwindled away slowly and intentionally, the joy of new life superseded by utilitarian logic. We have retreated from the sun, from the world outside. A world not dead by any means, just lesser, bland. Beauty was fragile. Resilience is compromise and lacks exuberance. The dandelion thrives. The orchid did not.

No, it is not fear that keeps us inside. We can only be swayed for so long by fear. At some point some portion of us will always set sail across the endless ocean to see if something is on the other side. Fear is something to be overcome. Shame though is paralyzing. To see the earth now is a sad affair, so we hide in our sky-lit houses of white, our lab-like greenhouses. The sky is still blue; we can pretend the rest remains unchanged.

We were waiting to fight an apocalypse, preparing for it all to end in fire, for only the strong to survive. So, when the realization came that life could go on, everyone just stumbled along with it, unaware of what we were giving up. I don't know how it all came about; no one found it notable enough to record.

Our world evolves still, but so slowly now; we have reached a stasis of sorts. In the heart of art and culture were stories we told ourselves, in one form or another. At their core stories were warnings, ways to express wisdom and plan for an unknown future. Our future stretches on, unchanging.

I set out to tell a story, but I may fail in that. Stories must have an end. I wonder now, despite our worst efforts, if we will ever end.

Jenna Muiderman

Astronaut

I stay here on my back for a while, staring at the sun behind the muted black and gold glass of the helmet. My head feels like cotton wool, but when I find a way to focus enough, the only emotion I latch on to is a placid bemusement. Eventually I lift my arms, testing the weight of the bulky suit. Back in the hospital, I had struggled to pull the book up to my eyes, my muscles stretching taut as piano wires. Now, although I can't see the state of my body beneath this suit, my arms rise without yielding to their own dull weight.

What page had I been on with that book? I remember the way the solicitor had looked at

it when I'd put it down to speak to her, the tattered
bookmark wedged between the fat block of pages, a
third in. The plot was heating up, but I couldn't read
fast enough, especially when solicitors kept coming
in talking about wills. And the parade of family members; some I hadn't even seen for a decade. What
was it now? Had there been a detective?

I drop my arms to my sides and fumble to prop
myself up on the sand. The gloves are so thick that
they feel more like paws, but they serve me well
enough. With some effort, I struggle to my feet.
Thinking it the polite thing to do, I pick up the
surfboard that lay next to me and tuck it under my
arm. I try not to think about it, nor question its
garish colours. The heavy boots anchor me and the
suit is so bulky that I bet there is no way I could
fall over; it would just stand up on its own. It makes
a change, I think, to the crunching quiver of my
usual walk. When I could walk.

I fumble at the visor of the helmet, but I can't find
a button to flip it open. Around me, a desert seems
to go on for miles; a rusty colour, even through the
visor's tinted glass. I scrabble at the helmet again but
it doesn't budge. My chest tightens. My breathing
is too close and quick. I smack at it. If Dad were here
he would tell me to think of something big and
open, but this desert is vast enough to swallow up
a scream.

I stab the surfboard into the sand and hold it tight,
rooting myself. The thin hiss of oxygen swirls inside
the helmet. There were times in the hospital when
an oxygen mask was pressed hard to my face. The air
was too pure: it pulled at my lungs and made me
dizzy. At first, I had not been able to catch my breath.

The nurse said it would help and, eventually, it did. But never as much as that book.

When I feel that I can breathe again, I heave the surfboard up, up out of the ground, and kick at the sand to show it who's boss. The particles are tiny and fade into a dust so fine that it seems to evaporate. Well, I think, I may as well head off. What else can be done?

I walk with slow, stomping footsteps, at first. It is hard to push the suit forwards; it protests against bending at the knee. But then I get the hang of it. Soon enough, I'm picking up some speed and turn to look at my footprints behind me.

'That's one small step for man.' I announce, tracking my way across the empty sands. My surfboard is heavier with each step, but in this suit I am strong. The sun blazes down from an empty blue sky, reflecting off the clinical white of the material. But I don't feel it. I'm cool, the oxygen humming around me. I pass the time by trying to remember that book. There was a detective in it, I'm sure. And someone was chasing something, maybe. I kept turning the pages and these bodies kept coming up, the way that they do. It was no longer enough to have just a little bit of intrigue in a mystery anymore; nobody takes it seriously until the body count rockets.

'You can't read that, love. Why don't you read something a little lighter?' My mum had said when she arrived with the usual batch of sherbet lemons and cards. She wore enough perfume to make my eyes water; protection against the antiseptic stink of the room. 'You know what I found in the attic the other day? *The wind and the willows.* You remember how you loved that? You used to dress up in your dad's waistcoat and jump around between the sofas, saying you were Toad of Toad Hall, you know.'

There must have been no recognition in my eyes because her face pinched together before I could say anything.

'You don't remember? You were such a little character, leaping about all the time.' Her voice cracked and she started to her feet. She suddenly needed the ladies. I didn't want anything to do with *The wind and the willows*, but I said, 'sure,' to keep her happy, and did the polite thing of ignoring how red her eyes were when she came back. I had never felt so constrained by etiquette as I did on that ward, which was quite an odd thing when you're peeing in a bag.

In any case, I kept the murder-book. I just pushed it into a drawer when my mum came around. I had even put a napkin between the pages of *The wind and the willows* for her, moving it on a few pages every day. I tried to figure out how long I had left. It was not a long book and I wanted to show that I would finish it before things ended. But not too early. I was afraid what Mum would produce once I had. Mr Men books, probably. 'You adored them as a child! They're cheerful.' I was sure she would say. Only, what she would mean was; 'nice and short.'

The desert seems to go on forever in every direction. I look back at my footsteps, squinting, trying to work out if I'm still going in a straight line. I'm no sailor; I have no idea how to orientate myself by the sun. Or if it is it even moving. How long have I been here? I study the horizon and pick out a large rock to aim for. I point the surfboard out, lining it up, and

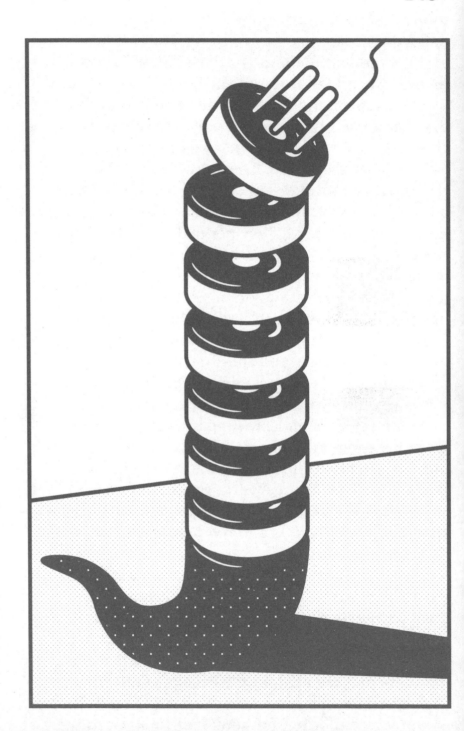

follow its nose. In the book, the main character
had a dog to do that sort of thing. It was a loyal mutt
and it would sniff about the dark alleys. It was
usually the dog that found the bodies, the detective—
what was his name?—he just dealt with the aftermath and tried to figure out why. I try to think of the
characters of each of the victims but draw a blank.
I know what they were: The sultry coffee shop dame,
the surly pawnbroker and, when I last placed the
bookmark, the noble police officer, but I don't really
know *who* they were. They popped up when convenient, but, really, they were just tropes. I imagine
myself slipped into that line-up: the patient. Maybe
it was not even a very good book. But I'd read it
like man drinks water in, well, a desert.

As I walk, I am not hot—that makes sense. But
neither am I thirsty and that frightens me.

The horizon is impossibly flat, but that boulder
sticks up in layered shards like a castle.

I keep my eyes on it, willing my feet forwards,
concentrating on the book. Things had been heating
up; the detective and his dog had the trail. But I
know how these things work, the big reveal wouldn't
come until the end. Up until then you had all these
alibis and motivations and red herrings to unpick.
Too clever for me.

On Mum's last visit I pulled out *The wind and
the willows*, with the napkin on the last page;
the pain had had a gnawing, cold feeling that day
and I thought it was a safe bet. She had seen it,
I was sure. I remember her hands on my face and
her tears pressed against my cheeks and I was
frightened to look her in the eyes. All I could think
about was that other, fat book half-finished in the

drawer. Why did the coffee shop dame, the pawnbroker and the policeman have to die? They didn't know each other. They were strangers, all of them. They'd done nothing but short change a few people, get lusty on the side, maybe take a bribe that they regretted. Human stuff. But they were strangers. Badly written strangers in a plot I was out of time to solve.

I kick my boot against the base of the rock and almost trip over, but I don't feel anything. I look down. I lurch with vertigo and almost drop the surfboard as I grab for the boulder. The horizon isn't a horizon, it's an edge. In front of me there is a sheer drop, the desert just a coating before a plunge of straight black rock that drops away into a blue expanse. More sky? I tilt my head this way and that, trying to compensate for the shading on the visor. I can make out the tiny crests of waves, far below. Up here, I can't hear anything but the hissing of the oxygen and yet I know that if I can just get close enough I will hear the ocean breathe.

I stand up straight and try to keep my balance. That addictive little book of cardboard cut-outs would still be in the drawer now. Perhaps someone will find it, read it and the detective and his dog will finally solve the case. The murders would have a point. The coffee shop dame, the pawnbroker, the policeman and the patient. That's how these stories work, even the badly written ones.

I step out to the edge, brandishing the surfboard like a shield.

I leap like Mr Toad.

Leanne Williams

Accountability

For Rick and Denise

Osi was an accountant. That's all he'd ever been.
A brief stint as a bank clerk, when he was seventeen
years old, but then everything changed and suddenly
nobody wanted to be bank clerks anymore. They
wanted to dress up in matching costumes and run
around making an awful mess of everyone else's
countries. So, Osi became an accountant. He was
very good, by all accounts. His boss called him
'the counting-frame'—*das Rechenbrett.* To his clients,
he was Herr Gröning. Osi's current client was the
German police. He had been asked to do battle with
the extensive records of a particularly difficult lady
named Frau Goldmann.

Frau Goldmann, the paperwork told him, was
from Stuttgart. A rich old widow. Her husband had,

predictably, been a jeweller. Frau Goldmann owned a fortune in diamonds, pearls, silver and so forth, which she had stashed away with the cunning of a schnapps-soaked, arthritis-riddled fox. Until, rather foolishly, she got herself arrested. A thorough investigation led the police to conclude that the old harridan had shipped them overseas. *She can't have been that clever,* thought Osi, *else she'd have shipped herself along with them.* Attempting to decipher the complex financial histories of the idle rich was arduous work—number-crunching, page-flipping, telephone-wrestling, pencil-chewing sort of work—but Osi was in his element. Frau Goldmann's misery was his intellectual delight.

'*Guten Morgen,* Osi.'

'*Morgen,* Max.'

'That old witch, eh?'

'*Ja.* Can't be long now. Coffee yet?'

'Not for another hour.' Max checked his watch. A beautiful piece. Perhaps by Herr Goldmann himself. '*Komm schon,* come! We can sneak a cigarette,' he said.

Outside, in the winter air, Osi and Max stood puffing away like two guilty schoolboys. Osi expected Richter to poke his ruddy *balloon* of a head out of the first-floor window at any moment. Max was too hysterical to care.

'...and then—guess what? No, really, guess what?'

'No idea, Max.'

'He started singing! Singing! The fat little flea started singing! I tell you, Osi, I've never seen anything so funny in all my life. I could have shit myself laughing, I swear!'

'What did he sing?'

'Oh, I can't say it!' Max's cheeks were bulging with half-swallowed laughter. 'I'd lose it if I told you!'

'You would,' Osi warned. 'You know better, Max. Remember Schaffer?'

'*Ja,* everyone remembers Schaffer. Who was his last client?'

'It doesn't matter. Just remember it was his last.'

'Roth! It was Roth! The old painter from Vienna.' The rich ones were always old.

'*Ruhe,* Max! Roth doesn't matter anymore. This time next week, Frau Goldmann won't matter either. You remember Schaffer.'

The missing punctuation hung in a curl of smoke. Max was quiet for a while.

'Yes,' he said soberly. 'Yes, I do.'

So the two friends smoked in silence until the stubs burnt their frostbitten fingers.

*

'Will the court please stand.' It wasn't a request. It was an order. Delivered calmly, elegantly, but with a subtle undertone of threat. *Please stand,* the voice said, *or we'll break your fingers.* I was used to hearing such voices. I heard them *wieder und wieder,* again and again, when I was an accountant. I'd always been an accountant. Herr Gröning, the accountant, *das Rechenbrett.* Like everybody else, I stood.

The judge came in. A portly *Mensch* who reminded me of Richter. The court waited patiently for him to stroll the five metres from the door to the desk. He moved with the slow majesty of a glacier—lofty and inevitable, holding the court in the ice of anticipation. My breath frosted.

'Herr Gröning,' boomed the judge. Nobody called me Osi anymore.

'*Euer Ehren,*' I replied, in a voice much smaller than I'd hoped for. Again with the ranks and titles; was 'Your Honour' so different from the rest? There was a ripple around the courtroom. Cameras flashed and sniggered.

'Herr Gröning,' he repeated, softer this time. He'd made his grand entrance. 'A most peculiar case.'

Was this an invitation for me to speak? His voice said yes, but his gunmetal eyes said no. I followed the eyes. Another thing I'd learnt as an accountant.

'Most peculiar indeed.' He was like a storybook character. Bearded, robed, and full of secrets. He was like the wise old wizard from *Star Wars*, from *Krieg der Sterne*, as they'd called it then. I'd watched it once, as a younger man. Not young enough. Good and evil, light and dark, right and wrong—it troubled me. Silly fantasy, of course, but always something more. 'May the court request an opening statement, Herr Gröning?'

Tell us, said his voice, *or we'll break your legs.*

'For me—' I began, and stammered. Was it really so hard? *Reiss' dich zusammen,* Osi! Pull yourself together. 'For me, there is no question that I share moral guilt.'

No cameras laughed this time. They'd stopped seeing the funny side. I'd struggled to find the humour in the first place.

'I ask for forgiveness,' I went on. 'I share morally in the guilt, but whether I am guilty under criminal law, you will have to decide.'

I glanced at Hans. Hans Holtermann, my defence lawyer. He looked as if he were watching Germany in the *Weltmeisterschaft* final. His glassy gaze was fixed on the judge as he mouthed the words we'd prepared together. I'd done that myself, many times, these last few weeks. In front of the *Spiegel* in my old house. The same mirror in which I'd once fixed my tie and combed my hair, polished my boots and straightened my cap, when I was an accountant. I'd always been an accountant. But did that make me accountable?

*

Osi's fingers were sore. The metal keys of a typewriter didn't take well to repeated hammering. Tomorrow, he would have bruises as well as frostbite. He pitied those who had to work outdoors. Still, there was always somewhere warmer.

He stood outside the main admin office. The same bland porridge-like wall, the same barrack-block lettering, the same symbol on the prison-cell door. The *Firmenstempel*, Richter called it—the company stamp. It had been a hard day's work, with little to show. Coffee, then lunch, then dinner had melted into an instant. They were well-fed, of course, given plenty of cigarettes and schnapps to stave off the cold. After all, they belonged to a very prestigious company. But try as he might, Osi couldn't make head nor tail of Frau Goldmann. He'd scribbled sheet after sheet of calculations, counted every last *Pfennig*, mustered his forces for the next assault. He saw it time and time again—a weak point, a chink in the armour, a hole in the walls of Babylon. With his arsenal of ink and lead, he poised for the killing blow... and, time and time again, he bounced harmlessly off the financial fortress of Frau Goldmann.

He knocked sharply on the door.

'*Ja?*' came a hedgehog voice from within.

'Gröning,' said Osi.

The door was flung open.

'*Komm' doch rein,* Osi!' beamed a lovely young blonde. Sore thumb was inadequate. Here was a rainbow in a sky still wracked with storms, a permed peacock in a cage of hens. 'Come in, don't be a stranger!'

'*Dankeschön,* Fräulein Hoppe.' He was married, she was not. Christian names simply weren't appropriate. There were stories in the office about the last receptionist. *Remember Schaffer,* he told himself. Christian names would be careless.

'Oh, *bitte!*' she whined. 'Call me Liesl. Everyone does.'

'I'm sorry, Fräulein Hoppe, but everyone shouldn't. I'm here for business.'

'You think I'm not?' she shot back.

'Touché,' Osi conceded. *Leave it there,* he thought. 'Well, Herr Gröning? How can I help you?'

Osi unclipped his briefcase—tan leather with sturdy metal clasps, someone else's name and address still faintly inked—and dug out a stack of typewritten sheets from under a copy of yesterday's *Observer.*

'I didn't know you were moving the Zugspitze, Herr Gröning. Or are you writing *War and Peace?*'

'You're a receptionist, Fräulein Hoppe, not the police.' A moment passed. 'Richter's pigeonhole, please,' he said hurriedly. Gone was the peacock—Liesl looked like a sparrow as she turned her back.

'Anything else?' Short and sharp.

'No thank you, Fräulein Hoppe. Not today.'

She walked him to the door. *Odd,* thought Osi.
He turned to say goodbye, but suddenly everything
was wild and flailing, was thunder and lightning,
was hair and perfume and shining sea-blue eyes. He
fell back against the doorframe as Liesl launched
herself onto him. She dug her nails into the back of
his neck. More bruises—maybe even cuts.

'I used to work in radio,' she growled. 'Then they
sent me here. Work for the *Firma*, they said. Better
pay, better food, better life, they said. They warned
me about some of the men, of course. But they
said nothing about the women and the children.
Oh, *Gott,* I wish I'd never left!'

Osi said nothing. He was just an accountant.
Liesl let him go. She looked ashamed. Terrified, even.
Eagle back to sparrow in the blink of an eye.

'I should be going, Fräulein Hoppe,' he stammered. The sparrow folded her wings in fear. 'We'll
say no more about it.'

From far away came the lonely whistling of a
train. As she shut the door, he noticed the tears in
her eyes.

*

'Would the first witness please stand?' asked
the judge. It was a question this time. I could tell.
No threat of violence, not for me. I had never
been an accountant. I looked at the man who had.
Counting, filing, stacking and scribbling—what
a life! He knew the price of everything, that man,
but did he know the value? Life. What was it
truly worth? Looking in *Der Spiegel* wouldn't tell
him. At least, not at the finance pages.

He was old. White-haired and wrinkled. Large tortoiseshell glasses on his nose. Woollen vest over a pressed white shirt. He looked frail and harmless. He looked like me. I didn't recognise him, I couldn't pick him out of a line-up. I had never seen Herr Gröning in my life. Yet nevertheless, here I was, just a once-young girl lost in time and space, being asked to testify against a man she never knew. He was just an accountant. Wasn't he?

'Please state your name and nationality,' said the judge.

'Eva Mozes Kor,' I said. 'US citizen, naturalised.'

'And your country of birth?'

'Romania,' I said. It sounded strangely foreign to me. '1934,' I offered, without invitation. I didn't feel I needed it.

I remembered everything. How could I not? To forget would be treason. I looked at the accountant. He could not meet my eyes. Did he recognise me? Impossible. We had never met in our lives. We had been close, within miles of each other at most. Yards, perhaps, maybe even feet. But our paths had never crossed. It wasn't right for us to meet in those years, in that place. The confrontation lay ahead, around the twists and turns of our snake-like lives, along the augured road that brought us both to Lüneburg *Landesgericht* in the April of 2015, to these plastic chairs and plywood desks of the future. My childhood world of wood and wool was gone. Consumed, eaten, swallowed whole by the demons of rubber and metal and glass. I remember the feel of them. The sight, the smell, the taste. The sounds. Hissing and humming, clattering and bubbling, the chords of a madman's symphony. Musicians came

and went, in surgical masks and spectacles. I was
only young. I don't remember the faces. But none,
I am sure, was the face of the man sitting before
me. Not one was the face of an accountant.

Does that make it easier? Knowing there is no
hatred I cannot feel, no vengeance I will be denied.
Nothing is beyond me now. I am here to bring
this man, finally, to account. I remember the faces
of my family. So long ago. So many others, whose
names I never learnt. There was no time. There
was no need. They took that from us. Israel and
Sarah, row upon row, name after name after name.
Numbers were what Herr Gröning dealt in, and
numbers were what we became.

Yet his name will be remembered. Not by many,
not for long. But it will. I see it now. He craves
anonymity. He craves numberhood, and the silent
oblivion it brings. He looks at me and wants rid
of his name. He would sacrifice himself, would see
himself obliterated, rather than carry his shame
any longer. He bears the cross of identity willingly,
perhaps even nobly. Yes, nobly is the word—like
a penitent eagle. He is more than just an accountant. He is human. Brave in his flaws, innocent in
his guilt, locked in mortal struggle against himself.
Aren't we all?

'And your connection to the accused?'

I say nothing. I need time. I see before me a man
who needs the same. Are we really so different?
He is to redemption as a fish to his water, is to
compassion as a lamb to her flock, is to forgiveness
as the birds to their sky. Without them, he will fade
into the night with the ink of time still wet upon
his cheek. Power surges through my veins. He is the

prisoner. I am the warden. The lost girl from Romania, dead at ten years old. I haven't been that child for seven times the span of her own meagre life. History hangs upon this moment, the inertia of the unthinkable balances on a pinpoint. I can tip the needle either way... How painfully Torahic. The accountant looks at me. He takes off his spectacles. Finally. Contact as close, as truly intimate, as anything I have ever experienced. *If you prick us,* ask his naked eyes, *do we not bleed?*

'Mrs Kor, I must repeat the question. What is your connection to the accused?'

'I was there,' I say, and the key fits the lock and it turns with a creak and the rusty cell door swings open in my mind and out steps an accountant, out steps a human being, out steps *SS-Unterscharführer* Oskar Gröning. 'I was at Auschwitz.'

*

Porridge-like wall, barrack-block lettering, that crooked cross of a *Firmenstempel*. Not the receptionist's office. This nondescript little cupboard was the lair of *SS-Untersturmführer* Moritz Richter, supreme overlord of the *Finanzabteilung KZ Auschwitz-Birkenau*, the extermination camp's accountancy department. Richter ruled his pen-and-paper empire with a grim passion. Under his scrupulous scrutiny, men, women and children were stripped down, split open and pulled to pieces, counted, weighed and measured, typed up, filed away and forgotten, melted into gold bullion, stamped with a swastika and loaded onto the very train they came in to go roaring into the hands of Walther

Funk and the vaults of the *Deutsche Reichsbank.*
From Berlin they were sent all over the Reich, to
the black smoke-and-steel cathedrals of industry, to
be made into guns and grenades, into aeroplanes,
artillery and armour, into bombs and battleships and
bayonets. To Moritz Richter, death begat death in
an extraordinary cycle of cause and effect. To Moritz
Richter, there was a beauty in the mathematics of
destruction.

Osi knocked three times.

'*Tritt' ein!*' Not the hedgehog voice of Liesl Hoppe,
but the staccato bark of a rifle.

Osi stepped into the office. A click of the heels and
a snap of the arm. Automatic.

'*Heil Hitler,* Herr *Untersturmführer!*'

'Is he sick?' grinned Richter, returning a half-
hearted wave. An awful and potentially fatal joke.
Protected by his authority, Richter was something of
a connoisseur. *Remember Schaffer.* Osi laughed
politely, but not so politely as to be rude.

'Did you receive my report on the Goldmann
accounts, Herr *Untersturmführer?*' asked Osi. He had
reluctantly handed it in almost a week ago. A
disappointing result, but so it goes.

'*Ja,* Gröning. I had a man from the Stuttgart
Gestapo telephone. They'd just about given up—no
thanks to you—when an air raid blew the old Yid's
house to shit. The clean-up team arrived, and *sieh da!*
There was her treasure, stashed in a wall cavity.
All that remained of it, anyway, smashed beyond all
hope of salvage. Slippery bitch. They were pleased
to know she was herself obliterated with Tuesday's
transport. Kapos said she made an awful racket.'

Osi didn't flinch.

'Didn't the *Gestapo* search the property when she was deported, Herr *Untersturmführer?*'

'*Na ja,* so they did. The officer who led the search is now rotting in Sachsenhausen.'

Clever old Jew, thought Osi. Staring death in the face, the stubborn Frau Goldmann had led her captors on one last dance. If it weren't for the British bombers, her treasure would have eluded Hitler forever. As it happened, he'd lost a considerable amount of pocket on the investigation alone, something the shattered pieces of jewellery would likely not recoup. Osi was just an accountant. He knew such things. He didn't want to know anything else.

Richter looked at him. There was something unspoken in that level stare. He knew, of course, why Osi was here. The Goldmann affair was a rare blip in the humdrum mundanity of the *Finanzabteilung's* everyday existence. Osi was back to tallying and typing the particulars of Auschwitz-Birkenau's less troublesome prisoners. Had been for a week, would be until they ran out of people to burn. Hours of finger-aching, brain-dulling, paper-scrunching boredom. But Richter knew that wasn't the real problem.

'Herr *Untersturmführer,*' Osi began. 'I was wondering if there had been any developments in regard to my previous request.'

He knew, and despite himself, he understood.

'Come now, *Rechenbrett,*' Richter sighed. 'You made a pledge. To *Führer und Vaterland.* Don't forget that there are always worse jobs to be had.'

Osi couldn't forget. He was just an accountant, but he'd seen it all—the head of a wailing baby smashed off the side of a truck; the pitiful whimpers

of the cripples, shot where they fell in blood and
filth; the faceless gravitas of the gas-masked man
as he emptied a tin of pellets into the iron hatch;
the humming, the screaming, the silence most
of all. He remembered the shrieking of the train-
whistles, the iron tread of jackboots and the
shouts of '*Raus! Raus! Raus!*'. He remembered the
night, late in '42, when the alarm had sounded
and they'd grabbed their pistols and gone hunting
Jews in the woods. He remembered the pit where
the bodies were burnt, the smoke and the stench
and the horror. He remembered the *Kapo*, who
had told him with grovelling pride how the whole
thing worked. He remembered how the bow-
legged creature with the gap-toothed grin had
slaughtered his brothers and sisters for a slice of
old sausage and a swig of schnapps. But Osi
was just an accountant. He too received his daily
bread. His family was in Germany.

'I'm afraid it's out of the question,' Richter
continued. 'Not at this stage. You're a good
accountant, Gröning. The *Finanzabteilung* needs
you. Here, you have better rations. Here, you
have books to read and beer to drink and friends
to play cards with. Here, you really are doing
the *Führer's* work. They're only Jews, Gröning—
what's conscience got to do with it?'

'Nothing, Herr *Untersturmführer*,' he said.

*

The *Prozess* was over. It had been nearly four
months. Today came the verdict. The co-claimant,
the survivor, had said her piece. So had sixty others.

Sixty! All here to testify against my client. All here,
so it seemed, to have their revenge. It's a terrible
thing, *Rache*. It burns you up like a fire from within,
leaving nothing but a twisted shell of a soul,
a scorch-boned skeleton with a pointing finger.
Trust me, I'm a lawyer.

It was always going to be a difficult case. Since
ninety-year-old Demjanjuk was convicted, a
precedent had been set. It was always going to be
difficult, but I took it on. Oskar Gröning. *Ja,* he
was just another fool of the times. His father was
in the *Stahlhelm*. He joined the Hitler Youth. He
went to book burnings and rallies, sang *die Fahne
Hoch* as loud as all the other little boys. How was
he to know, as a young man nursed on propaganda,
where the future would take him? Auschwitz
was Auschwitz. It can't be explained or forgiven.
Certainly not by Oskar, certainly not by me.
But since then, he's tried. The court ignored that.
They ignored all the efforts he's made. *Meine
Güte,* the man's spent years being harassed by those
who would tell him he didn't see what he saw,
didn't hear what he heard, didn't do what he did!
We've discussed it many times, this strange
phenomenon. The rejection of truth, the bitter,
reactionary denial. The obstinate perpetuation of
a disgraced and inhuman ideology. I can't understand it. Neither can Oskar. It's hard for him to live
such a life, but will they understand? *Nein.* To
them, he's just a Nazi.

Oskar's predicament is unique, no? Hated by
Hitler's supporters, hated by Hitler's opponents. He
can find no comfort here, with the gun-barrels of
a thousand cameras spitting electric venom in his

face. My client, I believe, has always fought a noble losing battle. Mrs Kor understood that. She, at least, offered him a chance. The irony. The bittersweet realisation. I don't see it very often. I see her now, sitting, hands folded in her lap. She looks composed, elegant almost, but there is an inner turbulence which only those who can read people may notice. I notice. Oskar doesn't. He worked with numbers, not people.

'Will the court please stand.' Not a question. We stand.

In comes the judge, that monolith of justice. His paunch seems to drag the rest of him towards his chair. There is no glacial grandeur this time. He is brisk and assertive. Professional.

'The jury of the *Landesgericht*,' he begins, pausing for effect. The cameras conjure up a perfect storm of *Blitzen*. 'Has reached a verdict.'

Mrs Kor smiles at me. A melancholy gesture, a compassionate offer to share in my anxiety. I return it shyly. *Mein Gott,* what a woman.

'This court finds the defendant, Herr Oskar Gröning...'

Time stretches. Seconds become hours. Colours, sounds, smells and shapes blend into an incomprehensible mess of nonsensical reality. An abstract painting. And who is the artist? Is it me? Judge Kompisch? Oskar Gröning? Mrs Kor? Who created this scene before us? What hand sketched the figures, held the brush, and mixed the paints? Perhaps it was all of us. Perhaps we painted this picture together. Both a landscape and a portrait, sweeping in its intricacy. Both classical and modernist, capturing time itself in all its joy and horror. I would

hang it in the Louvre, so everyone would understand. I would call it *The Essence of Innocence*. No—
I would call it *Accountability*.

'...*schuldig*...'

Guilty. The frame is shattered, the oil paint cracks
and the canvas withers away.

'...as an accessory to the murder of over 300,000
innocent persons, and receiving a sentence of four
years' imprisonment.'

Vier Jahre. Four! Oskar was 93 years old. They
could be the last four years of his life. They could
be an eternity. As the courtroom reeled and the earth
stopped still, Mrs Kor approached my client. The
Holocaust survivor stood before the former Nazi. She
embraced him. She kissed him. She thanked him.
Ach, *mein Gott!* That was fucking madness.

*

Osi took one last drag on his cigarette. He ground
it into the dirt. He had an appointment to keep,
at Lüneburg *Landesgericht* in just over seventy years.
He couldn't afford to be late.

'So, you're really leaving, eh?'

'*Ja,* Max. I'm going to the front. The Ardennes.'

'*Gratuliere,* Osi,' laughed Max. 'Send me a postcard,
won't you?'

The year was 1944. As Osi's train left Auschwitz
behind, another was pulling into the station. In a
carriage full of filth and corpses, clinging desperately
to her twin sister, was a ten-year-old girl from
Romania.

Aaron Saint John

Boxes

A: I know you did it.
B: I did not. You don't even know what it is you are accusing me of.

A: Yes I do.

B: No you don't. I defy you to rationalise your logic.

A: I love to rationalise all things.

B: I think you have a warped perspective of your own worth.

A: My favourite thing to rationalise is pie charts.

B: You've never come into contact with a pie chart.

A: Yes I have. I use pie charts all the time. In fact, I'm thinking of one right now. Guess which one.

B: *(the sound of thinking)* The correlation between sportsperson's earnings in relation to how likely they are to get away with rape or attempted rape?

A: No. But you were so close.

B: Oh was I?

A: Yes, you were.

B: I always am, but I never get first place. I'm not really a person who wins. I've never got a prize on a tombola and I've certainly never called full house at bingo.

A: I'm a really lucky person. I got five numbers on the lottery once.

B: What did you spend the money on?

A: I got myself a tombstone.

B: How lovely. What model? It's so hard to choose the right one, isn't it?

A: It's one of those shiny marble slabs and it's got a barn owl in the centre. I think everyone is really jealous of it.

B: I hate owls. They can kill a person, you know.

A: You've been listening to too many podcasts.

B: I haven't listened to any podcasts in fifteen years.

A: *(cross)* Bullshit. I hear you listening to them all the time.

B: That's your tinnitus.

A: Is that the one where you can't stop eating?

B: No. It's the one with the ringing in your ears.

A: I don't have any ears.

B: Do you not? I've still got mine.

A: I lost mine last year after that really bad frost.

B: Oh yes that was awful, wasn't it? Ester at the bottom gate lost all the skin from her arms.

A: *(shocked and sad)* But Ester was so pretty.

B: Well, she's not anymore. Her suitors have dwindled somewhat. She's very upset about the prospect of being unattractive.

A: You can't be beautiful forever; that's not how it works around here. And you know what it's like. There's always a flock of interest when a new one moves in. Ester's not fresh meat on campus anymore.

B: Well of course not; she's got no arms.

A pause occurs for an indeterminate period.
It could be a minute, hour or lifetime.

A: Are you sure you didn't do it?

B: For heaven's sake, how many times do I have to tell you? I didn't do it!

A: *(pause)* I know you probably didn't. I just like being reassured. It's a very comforting feeling.

B: *(sighing)* Do you want me to tell you?

A: Yes, please.

B: But you never remember.

A: This time I promise I will.

B: It was a motorbike accident.

A: *(incredulous)* A motorbike accident? I don't even like motorbikes.

B: *(patiently)* You did. You liked them very much.

We used to talk about them a lot when you first
got here.

A: But motorbikes are so dangerous.

B: Apparently when you were alive you didn't seem
to think so.

A: *(fascinated)* How curious.

Another pause

A: The worms are eating my brain aren't they?

B: Most likely. I don't think your coffin was closed
properly.

A: That will be Sarah, she always liked cutting
corners. My pillow is horrible in here.

B: She came to see you a couple of weeks ago. She
brought her current husband by the sound of it.

A: Oh yes. I think he's a quantity surveyor. Nice guy.

B: I didn't like the way he was dismissive of your owl.

A: People are entitled to their opinions. Not everyone
can like owls.

B: I got the impression he would have criticised
whatever was on there. Be it owls or any other
member of the animal kingdom.

Pause

A: What do you think happens after here?

B: I don't follow.

A: Do you think we've got anywhere left to go? Or is
this it?

B: I don't think we are supposed to ask these kind of
questions. Questions never solve anything. They
only lead to more questions.

A: I wish I had asked to be cremated.

B: Why?

A: Because I would have asked to be thrown into the ocean and gone on adventures.

B: You might have got eaten by a fish.

A: It's better than being stuck here waiting for a second death.

B: You are very negative today.

A: *(gloomily)* Yes, I think I might be depressed.

B: You should see a doctor.

A: I might. Do you think they will give me drugs?

B: Probably, I know Bert next to the fountain gets pills for his Parkinson's.

A: I don't like Bert.

B: Now you are just being cruel.

A: I don't like him because he laughs at people that haven't been buried in a suit. That's cruel.

B: He's just of a different era. Things were more formal back then.

A: I heard he had intimate liaisons with the KGB.

B: From who?

A: His next door neighbour. She said he always has some really shifty-looking visitors on his anniversary and one of them carries a gun.

B: Who's his neighbour?

A: Delia. You know, the one with the eye.

B: Delia hasn't uttered a grain of truth in twenty years. She'd be the one with the spy ring, not Bert.

A: My world's been turned upside down. I don't know what to believe anymore. My head hurts.

B: *(softly)* Why don't you go to bed? It's getting late.

A: How do you know?

B: I've just got a feeling it's late in the day. That's all.

Rebecca Sandeman

The man in my margins

I pick up a book from the library. She has not been asked out on a date since 2010. Before that it was 2003. I wonder if she is unhappy that she has spent her good years being left there on the shelf, alone and unchosen. Everyone wants to read Sylvia Plath. She's always going out on dates, sometimes for a week or more. I bet she has lots of pages with creases along the top corners. I bet she has plenty of things underlined. I bet that *Daddy* is covered in pencil hearts and undergrad biro. I'm not saying that Sylvia is a floozy but I wager she's been in plenty of twenty-year old girls' bedrooms, boys too. She has probably sat on many a nightstand and watched terrible three am kisses and knickers being thrown across the room with misguided tenderness. Sylvia has seen it all. But my book hasn't. She has to beg all the other books for details when they come back—that's if they come back at all. You know how fickle people can be when it comes to returning things that aren't theirs.

Frank O'Hara has the best stories. And so does Jack Kerouac. Even Ted Hughes does, at least once in the year, in the right circumstances. Frank went to a warehouse rave recently and got read out for fifteen minutes at an after party when dawn was streaming through some net curtains. They did lines of MCAT off his hardback cover and his date, a nineteen-year-old techno enthusiast called Melvin, defended Frank when someone wanted to rip one of his pages to inhale drugs. It was his finest hour. Everybody really enjoyed Oranges, even though they were really gurney. Frank has been the coolest book on the entire floor since then. Barbara Guest has been fangirling over him but he's not that interested. He's in love with Flannery O'Connor but won't admit it. And she got moved to a lower level because of an inept librarian; he pines from a distance and loves from a great height.

I took my new book home. I'd hired her for an entire seven days. I could feel her shivering in my bag with nerves the whole way back. I imagine she wanted to know what I planned to do with her. She was mine to spread open as I so wished. I think she was a little frightened but I reassured her that I intended to use her for an essay on Lethargic Romantics, she could teach me things noone else could. It didn't matter if she was a little rusty or out of shape. We could go at her pace. No pressure to do everything immediately. I wasn't like all the others.

The next day I came to her early in the morning and cracked her spine. She made that satisfying sound of the unspoiled canvas. I brought my nose

up to her middle and took a long deep sniff: she was
perfect. Her blank, white flesh was a silk camisole
in my hands. I lifted her gently on to the kitchen
table and began to have her, I took her mind, ideas
and body and ate them without pause for breath.
She could no longer speak but I could speak for her,
she was in ecstasy having been chosen at last and
by me. It was the fourth chapter when I saw him, the
man in my margins. I know I said I was going to be
gentle, but she was so good I couldn't stop myself
from gorging. I threw her onto the tiled floor and she
cut her head.

'Who the fuck is he?' I screamed. 'Who the fuck
has written all over you, tainting you with his
rancorous words?'

I picked her up by the hair and smashed her skull
into the floor again. She was bleeding and screaming for someone to help her. But her friends couldn't
hear, they were all back in the library preening,
thinking only about themselves or Frank.

'You come across as an innocent, virtuous book,
but you are just the same as the rest of those sluts.
Why do you think I chose you in the first place?
You aren't even that pretty, your cover art is awful.'

I left her on the tiles until mid-afternoon.
I skirted around her discomfort and made myself a
Mediterranean vegetable flatbread. I read other books
in front of her, books who were pure and without
the diseased thoughts of others scrawled across their
breasts. They could offer me more than she ever
could, but her body was flailed at a delicate angle
and the vulnerability was bewitching. I crawled back
over to my dormant, injured princess and let her
weep on my compliant thigh.

'Please don't cry my sweetheart,' I cajoled,
stroking her matted mane. 'I'm sorry that
we have perceived each other in such a way that
was unrepresentative of our intrinsic characters.'

She continued to cry, my knees began to
get rather wet. I told her to stop because she was
at risk of blurring herself with tears and then
nobody would be able to understand her. She was
in danger of becoming indecipherable and of no
purpose; a book without words is no use to
anyone at all.

'Can I see him?' I averted my eyes from the
impending mess. 'Love makes marks on us all you
know. And often you can't just erase it with stuff
you find in the stationary shop bargain bin. Tippex
can remove indication of memories but not the
actual memories themselves. In fact, the sheer act
of erasure draws attention to the remembering;
you can't forget to remember that you need to forget.'

She ceased her sobbing and looked a little
puzzled, but the profundity of my tone ensured
she didn't question me with her mouth; it was just
the flicker of her eyes that told me of her doubt.
Disapproval is manageable, even encouraged, if told
through the windows of your soul. What I can't
abide is challenges to my integrity through the me-
dium of the sentence. Sentences are abrasive and
nonsensical. They are of ill repute and belong
to the classes concerned with savagery and change.

Slowly, but hesitantly, she fell open to expose
her imperfections. She was tattooed from top
to bottom with the hieroglyphics of a foreign being;
her navel had a chicken scratched lyrical ballad
which looked like Keats' musings post-death mask

and pre-St. John's gates. A transitory period if you will, of monumental clarity and indulgence into the self. A self that was not hers.

It must be hateful to carry the opinions of others on your shoulders and bear the brunt of the weight they inflict. Opinions that wrench and twist the graphite composition of your watercolour silhouette. Pens are the most destructive weapon invented by man, not bombs. Bombs topple buildings but pens topple countries and regimes so there is nothing left but the swirling dust of dictator ash. But it's only ever the dictators that tend to claim the historical narrative. A history book would be awfully dull if it concentrated on the victims; a list of beige names does not fascinate or entice. What can be learnt from the dead who didn't hang around long enough to find justice? Who can truly feel sorry for those not equipped with enough pens or bombs to survive a harsh nuclear winter? Radiation sickness is a fallacy; people die because they are sick of the feebleness inside their own black, browbeaten hearts.

Neither of us needed to speak, we understood each other perfectly. No-one should be punished for scars cut with careless knives that haven't had the opportunity to heal.

'Are you sure it's what you want?' I asked her. 'Once it's done it can't be undone.'

She nodded. The stoic finality of her gesture combined with the black and white tiles of my kitchen made her look so breathtakingly beautiful. It was the way the blood in her hair caught the last of the afternoon sun. I was utterly enchanted. I fell in love with her all over again. I no longer even cared about Lethargy and The Romantics. The aftermath of distress creates an atmosphere exceedingly rich in sticky pheromones and fluid. I think that's often why soldiers caught up in war feel the strong compulsion to rape. Sorrow can be a supple emollient more effective than any mint-tingling lubricant found on the weekly shop and hastily thrown into the trolley, next to a pack of peach probiotic yogurts.

The rubber was a small brick in my palm. I think it had once been used to build mountains which had been unduly silenced by hate. I told her to take a deep breath in and count to ten. I wasn't sure if the friction or the eradication of pencil opinions might cause an awkward, throbbing sensation, like chlamydia. She complied and I began to erase all traces of him, the man who had come before me and ruined her.

A lobotomy occurred that day on my floor in the fading light. I was a doctor that held the tools of rebirth in my unwashed hands. She was born into a world of decay and unrepentant sinners at 6.47pm. I cut the cord of her former life and she fell unburdened and amniotic into my lap; she did not know her name or mine, but it was fine, she could learn life with a clean slate. That was my gift to her, purity is not something you can order off Amazon Prime or to be post through stiff letterboxes, like Christmas cards to acquaintances you aren't fond of. It was something you earned through hard work and diligence—from restraint and layers of pale petticoats under microscopes.

She had been returned to her home not four days when there was a knock at the door. We had parted on good terms, I thought. She gave me a lingering kiss on the cheek before I gave her back

to the librarian with the bad cardigans. The CCTV
will attest to that. It was the police. I was arrested
on my doorstep and charged with grievous bodily
harm, rape, attempted rape and kidnapping, which
is ridiculous because she went with me of her own
free will; it's her job to be used. I'm looking at
seven years; my lawyer thinks I need to cut a deal.
They've got DNA and testimony and witnesses.
Apparently, my next-door neighbour saw something
ghastly when she went to water her hydrangeas in
her dressing gown. And this is all because I wanted
to learn. She lied and lied to me and now I shall rot
in a cell because she pretended to be someone she
never was. People should come with warning labels;
it shouldn't be up to me to expose the fractures
in their psyches, if you go into the borrowing profes-
sion don't borrow narratives that aren't yours to
claim. It makes me laugh that a lady of the archive
night thinks she's worthy of reporting a crime
that's steeped in sex. Needless to say, they've taken
my library card and I'm not allowed within 500 m
of a bookshop. It's a real shame because I have lots
of Waterstones' points that run out in June. And
they've confiscated the contents of my shelves to
protect the safety of other stories. I think they want
to put me on a register. There is no joy left in my
life now, she has taken everything from me that I
once held dear. My brain matter and sanity decrease
by the hour and all I can do is await my fate and
watch episodes of *Tipping Point* and *Judge Rinder*.
I hold mugs of cold, bitter tea and often wish that
I was dead.

Rebecca Sandeman

Census

I found my lover's body twisted out of shape like
a piece of modern art. His breath was short and
strained. When he saw me, he gurgled, words becoming bloody bubbles at the corners of his mouth.
I knelt down by his knotted form and tried to find
somewhere familiar I could hold, but the pavement
had forced all familiarity from his body. His legs
had invaded the space formerly occupied by his
torso, causing his arms to wrap around and within
themselves in form of compromise to allow for
the shifting of space. He turned his face away from
me despite causing his entire body to convulse
in pain, all just to hide his embarrassment of his
botched suicide attempt.

'Ryan, I'm going to get you help ok, you're
going to be fine.' He had obviously misjudged the
height of the roof of our building and hit the ground
with an impact only strong enough to contort his
being. Ten floors were plenty for living the high life
but not ending it.

I took my hand and placed two fingers below
what was left of his chin and turned his face back
towards me, not caring of any extra pain I was
causing him. I'd never seen him look scared before.
Now I could tell from his eyes that he wasn't
scared of dying but of living.

'They made me remember... I can't... I can't...' I
heard him say beneath the bubbles. I knew there was
no point in trying to save him, not even to reassure
him. Once they force you to remember there's no
going back. I took my fingers from his shattered jaw

and placed them around his oddly fine nose and squeezed. I placed my other hand around his throat and tightened it, feeling bones snap and cartilage pop beneath my fingers. When I was sure he was dead, I left his body where it had landed and returned to our flat knowing his body, along with every record, every notion him, would be gone by morning.

His letter was waiting for me on the kitchen table. I opened it and picked up the first book I could reach. Without actually taking in the content of the letter, I underlined each word he had used in the book in the order he had used them. All that I left out were our names. When I had done, I tore up the letter and set it alight on the hob and waited.

It was 2.00am when they knocked on my door with their piteous smiles and black armbands over green sleeves. I let them shuffle in, accepting their condolences with silence before shutting the door behind them. I stood in the bedroom doorway and without looking at them I said: 'I'd like to remember him if that's alright,' before getting into bed and leaving them to work.

*

It started as a personable way for the government to collect information. They would knock on your door, dressed in their green blazers and their smiles, and ask if the time was right for you. If it wasn't they would come back when convenient and if no time ever was, you would never see them again. But most people let them in—there was something about their smiles you just couldn't deny—and soon kettles would be on, biscuits would be out and you would talk. When they had everything they needed, they would pack up and go, never outstaying their welcome or being too quick. They would leave when it was just right.

The information they collected through these chats began as fairly standard issue: religion, wage bracket, the harmless things the government liked to know. As the myth of terror grew more persuasive, however, so too did the questioning: 'Do you feel safe? What are your opinions on the refugees?' Of course, the questions were rarely that blunt, they would arise as naturally as they would in the pub and answers would never be explored or debated, just accepted. More and more intelligence was being gathered and nobody noticed. With all the issues surrounding online privacy, no one thought anything about face to face privacy. People were just glad to have somewhere other than a computer screen to share the most mundane corners of their lives.

No one knows for certain when they started taking secrets. By the nature of it, no one can really remember giving them; at most you would remember they had visited and have some vague feeling of release. Word spread before it became official; the census would listen to you, to things you don't want to feel or remember, and they would take them away.

They called it absolvement. It was based on the idea of the confessional, picked from the remains of the Catholic Church, meaning whatever you told them was confidential. Even if they took abhorrent memories away from you: murder, paedophilia, they would do nothing other than free you from the burden. Until you stepped out of line.

It turns out dangling an individual's darkest flaw in front of them is an excellent form of coercion. If you take away a person's guilt they will do whatever you ask of them and, if they don't, you only have to threaten to give it back.

Now nearly everyone has been absolved, even me. Obviously, I can't remember what for and I don't want to remember, because most who are forced into reminiscens disappear. Some commit suicide, some end up in prison; some, like Ryan, fuck it up and have to hope someone who loves them is there to finish them off. After the initial action, they come back in their green blazers, with added black armbands and a sombre smile, and remove every piece of evidence of that person's life. Even their memory if asked.

I didn't want to forget Ryan because something didn't feel right. In truth, he was boring. So the question wasn't what he had remembered, but why he was reminded. What had he done that made the census interested in a random accountant in the city?

*

The sun woke me the next morning. My body was the same aspirational foetus it had been when I went to bed. I left the apartment without looking at anything. I stopped for a coffee on my way to the office and drank it in a park feeling oddly fine.

There had been a subtle shift in the office. Everything felt normal but misplaced. Amy always asks me about Ryan but instead her conversation went straight to summer plans. Then there was

Todd who asked me if I wanted to go for a drink after work, just the two of us. I declined.

My office appeared untouched but I could tell they had been by a pile of misplaced files in the centre of the desk. When they performed an erasure on someone's existence they didn't leave any official documentation. To leave evidence of an erasure would be a paradox. Instead they would politely let whoever remained know that they had been by leaving something obviously out of place. I had only been in my office for a few weeks so there wasn't much in there anyway. I tried my best not to think about a completely empty office across the city; clean scabs on dusty concrete walls where framed pictures will have been torn off.

The only personal item I have in my office so far is a framed photo. I spent my morning focusing on tasks away from it; reading files and chasing people up. I didn't look at it until lunchtime. If anyone had looked at it yesterday they would have seen me and Ryan arm in arm above a mountainous vista. Today they would only see me, smiling by myself with my arm sticking out at an awkward angle.

But because I chose not to forget him I could see something different. At first my eyes were only drawn to me but as I stared harder I could make out the shape of something else. It was like the photo had been physically folded, trying to halve him out of the pictures' reality. His body had crumpled and his face had changed, as if his eyes had been moved further apart, his nose lowered and his lips shrunk into his chin. It was barely recognisable as a face let alone his. When you choose to remember a reminiscens casualty the only place they are allowed to continue to exist is in your memory. All physical remains of them are erased completely. This means the bereaved never complain, never fight back. It's hard to hold up a martyr only one person can remember.

Once I was aware of the photo I stopped paying the day the attention it craved. I made myself look busy by pretending to sort through files until I could leave. I remember on my way back I stared at the people I passed wondering how large a mark they had made on the world and how easy it would be to scrub out.

Back at the flat I was struck by how quiet it was. We were never a loud couple but now there was more space on the walls for the silence to echo. My first act was to take all the photos and put them in a drawer, just like in the office. To get rid of them seemed like a betrayal but to look at the swirled features of each one would be nauseating. I surveyed the rest of the flat, wanting to inspect every fresh patch of skin after its treatment. I wanted to find my pain for Ryan in the spaces he left. But instead I needed to know his reason so I went straight to the bookshelf and picked up the book containing his letter.

On the whole, it was self-defacing, apologetic and sentimental. *I can't go on knowing and this way it won't affect you.* Whatever he remembered must have been from a long time ago. When I knew him, he hadn't done much worth remembering let alone forgetting and they say the longer you're absolved from something, the harder it is to live with again. There was one sentence I didn't understand. *Those streets are still safe.* Irritated by it I left the book and paper on the breakfast bar and went to introduce myself to my new-old life.

Any items that were obviously just Ryan's had been taken, along with a few shared items, only to be replaced with something almost identical. It reminded me how big the flat was. You might not be able to measure a person by their possessions but it's certainly a good way to measure their absence.

The only items that had been left that weren't mine was an assortment of maps Ryan had recently gotten into collecting. The census sometimes misses the odd small thing; an infallible attempt to seem fallible... As the only physical remains of him I sat down and studied them, tracing their lines as if they were the cracks of his skin. They were all of the same busy area of the city—not far from where he worked—going back several years. The maps had grown more concentrated over time as streets were imagined out of existence. In one map what was a wide-open street was lost in the compression between two rows in a later one.

If they could make you forget a person, why not a place as well? Finding the maps scared me. I wish they hadn't missed them, but they had. Captivated, I reached for the letter: *Those streets are still safe.*

*

It seems the best way to kill a street is to erase all knowledge of it.

The city must be littered with packets of space that don't appear on any map, GPS, or even by sight. Even if you were to absent-mindedly wander into one you would start to feel as if you had entered some kind of void. All sense of place would leave and you would give in to an overbearing instinct to turn around and walk back toward the living. Or at least you would if you weren't fearless like Ryan was.

He would spend his lunch breaks walking. He loved his office and his job but felt to truly appreciate it he needed to get out when he could. So, every weekday at 12 o'clock, he would set off. I had thought the walking and the maps were just dull, eccentric habits. If I'd known they had been connected and where they would lead, I might have tried to stop him.

I don't know which came first for him: the walking or the streets. I presume that one day he just found himself on one and just decided to carry on walking. I don't for one second think he was doing it out of some radical notion, he was probably just interested in the architecture. But being the only thing that could put him on the radar of the census I had to look into it, to follow his stupid footsteps.

The maps varied a little but each contained one area that seemed especially interesting. It was once a circular plaza that had seven streets leading to it. It was only a short distance from where Ryan worked and was surrounded by shops, hotels, businesses and one of the city's iconic markets. As the maps got newer though, streets were vetoed until only one remained. Ryan must have chosen to explore where he wouldn't be noticed slipping away. There he must have found something he shouldn't have and was caught doing so.

*

I went one lunch hour. It was an ordinarily pleasant day and the plaza was teeming. Tourists swatted around taking pictures and workers sat with their jackets off, eating lunch talking loudly about business. It was clear no one else was aware of the conjoining streets; even I could barely spot them. Without thinking about it I threaded myself through and crossed the threshold. My muscles tore at me to turn back but I forced myself to carry on. There was nothing peculiar about the street beside its emptiness. Above me towered a metropolitan hotel. Red velvet flags hung moulding in the breeze; lanterns on the wall were filled with rainwater. Through the frosted glass, I thought I was being watched. There must be people that take refuge in places like this. People who were forced to remember or people who just chose not to forget.

Other elements had been disturbed. There were posters and bits of graffiti, all connecting to a counter-culture Ryan must have encountered. He had always had a thing for lost causes, they wouldn't have had to try very hard to seduce him. When I figured this out I turned, wanting to leave without being dragged into the mess Ryan had contaminated himself in.

As I turned to run I noticed a larger section of graffiti on the wall behind me. *It isn't just our secrets they hide* blazoned in big red letters on the beige concrete. My breath froze in my throat and cut into my mouth and I started sweating acid. I could hear footsteps approaching me, wanting to drag me further in so I ran whilst I still could. All this had made me suffer enough by losing Ryan's life without taking mine as well.

I emerged onto the plaza from behind a phone box gasping for clean air. The rest of the world had continued as normal. I looked at everyone wondering if they would want to know what I had found out. I envied their ignorance.

As I looked around I made eye contact with two men in green blazers. I tried to escape their gaze by making my way around the plaza but their eyes followed me, never pausing and barely blinking. They knew what I had seen and they would be coming for me. I collapsed into my knees, sweat mingling with tears. When I regained my composure, they were still there, watching me from the same spot. They wouldn't take me now, they don't like making a scene. I nodded at them, and started making my way out of the plaza through the living street and headed back towards the flat.

*

I sat in the darkness waiting for them to appear. They were either going to force me into a reminiscence or, if what I had been absolved of wasn't horrifying enough, they would do something worse. In the flat the prospect of becoming just another absence after an erasure felt too real, so I headed up to the roof.

Three days ago, I woke up and my life was fine but only because I couldn't know if it was any different. If I had known where all of this could end would I have just forgotten him? Life would have been good again, it would have been life. But now ten floors up I wondered if I deserved all this; whether I was guilty not for what I might end up remembering, but for having chosen to forget in the first place...

Chad Bentley

Lottie

'I pop pop pop blow blow bubble gum.
You taste of cherryade.'

For a while, I got by living on nothing but air. It wasn't easy and in London, like any big city, nobody goes out of their way to give you a leg up. And I must have looked awful too, because not even the Jehovah's Witnesses and Mormons on the street would approach me. But I got by.

As it happened, I eventually did get a call to work at an event one night. That's how the Gourmet Food Company rolls: they only call when they need you. And actually it's you who have to call them most of the time to remind them that living on nothing but air isn't so easy.

The event was apparently some kind of function for diplomats and businesspeople. We got there early to unload the glassware, plates, cutlery, table-cloths, wine, chairs, flowers, vases, crate after crate of champagne. Everything a guest could possibly require.

The Gourmet Food van had the company logo printed on the side: a red tomato, which from a distance could be mistaken for a pulsating heart in a pool of blood.

The places they catered for were amazing though. I got to see the inside of the Saatchi Gallery, The British Museum, Two Temple Place, the Round

House... That day it was Australia House I got to see. Inside there were huge round columns leading to the domed ceiling with glass chandeliers. The whole building had an Ancient Greek mythological vibe about it.

'You guys have five minutes to get your stuff on,' said James, the boss.

We all went to get changed into our work gear: black slacks with white shirts bearing the tomato on the breast pocket, our waists wrapped in white aprons.

As the girls tied back their hair, some of the guys twisted wax and gel into theirs.

After an hour or so, the room was brimming with white-haired guests in eveningwear. I did the rounds with a tray of champagne flutes. I had to dodge some of the guests as they hobbled around unsteadily and came close to losing the whole tray of glassware once or twice. Every now and then I had to change the tray from one arm to the other to avoid them going numb.

One of the new guys asked me if we were allowed to accept tips. He was tall and had an athletic build. His name was Daniel.

'Only if they're not expecting something from you in return.'

Later on, one of the silver-haired ladies spilled her glass of wine all over my white apron. I got Daniel to take my tray and headed for the lifts. As I was walking through the reception hall, it occurred to me that most of the houses in London were at least a hundred years old and Australia House would be no different. In Peru they'd have been a big deal, but here you took it for granted.

I felt classy and kind of important, enjoying the contrast of my lustrous black shoe leather against the immaculate white stone. I went down a level, took off my apron and saw the large wet patch on the front of my trousers. I went into one of the toilet stalls nearby and began using the hand dryer to sort it out. After a while I sat down on the lid of the toilet and rested my head on the cistern. It was cool.

I don't know whether it was because I was tired, hungry, bored or a combination of all of them, but I'd fallen asleep and was startled awake by someone banging on the cubicle door. I swung the door open and saw the pale faces of Daniel and the boss, James. James was an ok guy but totally unforgiving with this kind of thing. I was fired on the spot, which was what Daniel clearly intended to happen going by the look on his face.

I quickly got changed, threw my work clothes into my backpack and put on my white Pumas.

As I was heading for the exit I caught sight of Daniel, who still looked pleased with himself.

He had taken my place in the pecking order after all.

'I don't know what's worse, not having a job or being a dick.'

He stopped to think about it and finally replied, 'Not having a job, I'd say.'

I kept on down the hall towards the main entrance. I was the only one in trainers and jeans and now just felt like an impostor. I stopped to serve myself the last of a Moet & Chandon into a plastic cup. The dinner conversations of hundreds of guests echoed around me in a haze. I took a sip from the cup and continued on my way through the entrance hall and out onto the street. There were crowds of people hurrying by, scuttling off in all directions. Like an infestation of ants.

I wondered where the hell all these people had managed to find work.

I crossed the street and was continuing along The Strand in the direction of Charing Cross Station when I realised a metallic green Jag was cruising along next to me. The driver was waving and calling me over. I thought it must have been someone looking for directions. An ant that had lost its way. As I approached, the window sunk smoothly into the side panels. It was her at the wheel—twice my age but, as I came to learn, still a girl at heart.

I looked her over. She was wearing a steel-grey evening dress and her plunged neckline was adorned with dark olive-like stones. Her green eyes were calm and open. It had been a long time since a stranger had looked at me so openly and welcoming, in a way that's unusual in Europe.

'Hello... Can I help you?' I asked, almost like I was still working.

She adjusted suede gloves. 'Look, I am moving house shortly and was planning to leave this TV in a charity shop. I wonder if you could use it?' She signalled with her eyebrow towards an enormous plasma lying on the backseat.

'What do you want for it?'

She opened the passenger door. 'Hop in'.

She was smiling.

I jumped into the car. The seats were cream-coloured leather and there was a smell I found relaxing, like a mixture of sandalwood and cinnamon.

I could see her legs bare from the knee down where the skin was soft and fresh. I could feel she was beginning to notice my gaze so I turned and looked out the window.

'By the way, my name is Charlotte,' she said. 'But everyone calls me Lottie'.

'I'm Fernando,' I replied. 'My friends call me Nano.'

'Ok. Nano.' she said thoughtfully. 'I feel awful about what happened to you in Australia House. It was my aunt that spilled the wine on you'.

'Don't worry about it,' I said. I couldn't believe I hadn't noticed her at the party. She was beautiful.

I asked her if I could turn on the radio. I wanted to distract myself from thinking about everything that had just happened at The Australian Embassy, the spilled wine, getting fired. I found the signal for Radio 4. There was a woman leaving a voicemail for someone named Andrew, begging him to call her. Love unrequited.

'How can you listen to *The Archers*? You're not old enough to listen to radio dramas,' Lottie laughed. 'Look in here, Nano, I have some CDs instead,' she said, opening the glove compartment.

I pulled out the first disk and put it on. There was a picture of a woman with her head in her hands on the front cover of the CD. KT Tunstall. The music came through the speakers with a fidelity that I had never heard in a car before.

'Oh 'cause I'm under the weather,
Just like the world,
And I need somebody to hold
When I turn out the light.

You're out of sight,
Although I know that I'm not alone
Feels like home.'

We had gone past Victoria Station and were heading towards Chelsea when it began to rain. *Figures,* I thought to myself, *in London.* The rain, together with the glass of champagne and the voice of the girl singing began to bring me down a little. Eventually Lottie parked the car in front of a white Georgian terrace. We sprinted towards the doorway in an effort to keep ourselves dry, without much success. She pulled out a handful of keys. The wind was hurling the rain into our backs. She got the door open and pulled me inside, where she looked at me and took me by the hand. Her hair was soaked through and her skin was cold and smelled like cinnamon. Like a mother walking a child to school, she led me to the master bedroom where we immediately gave expression to what was so rapidly bringing our lives together. There was an air of sadness in her room, but there is nothing better for sadness than making love. It felt as if the world were about to fall to pieces and this was our answer.

'Do you…like me?' she asked, as we lay in bed.

'What do you mean?'

'Do you think I'm…attractive?' she clarified, slightly embarrassed.

'Very,' I said. 'You look like an Elizabethan actress.'

'Because I'm old or overly dramatic?'

'No, no, not at all. Because you're lovely. You're beautiful.'

It was all a bit strange, having gone from total strangers to fresh lovers so rapidly.

'But…'

'I like you, Lottie. I want you.'

The next morning, I woke up with light streaming in through the window and no sign of Lottie. On a nightstand next to me there was a photograph of her, much younger. In the photo she was wearing a ridiculously oversized hat that somehow she still made look elegant. There were also two books by PG Wodehouse, *Summer Moonshine* and *Cocktail Time* and another thick volume with flowers on the cover called *Poem for the Day.* I flicked through them for a while, but soon grew bored.

I got up and went to the window. Lottie looked up from outside and waved. She was preparing a table for breakfast. The garden was large and there was a horse sculpted from white stone in the centre. There were vines burgeoning at the side-walls and at the back two trees, guarding the oasis like sentinels.

'Were you comfortable last night?' she asked, serving tea.

'Very.'

She passed the sugar. 'I'm feeling a bit over-whelmed. Happy, but a little… nervous. It's a mix of emotions.' She exhaled deeply and continued. 'I'm just getting old I suppose. I should probably start taking a yoga class or something.'

'You have a beautiful body.'

'You're sweet, Nano. Thank you.'

After breakfast, she walked him through the garden. She was wearing a blue dress with white spots that perfectly contained her figure. Without making eye contact, she said 'You probably think I'm crazy. Picking you up off the street and taking you to bed like that.'

'No,' I answered, although the thought had occurred to me. 'I do wonder why you wanted to though.'

'I don't want you to think I do this all the time,' she said, finally turning to look at me. 'But when I saw you last night with that tray of champagne...I felt as if we'd already knew each other.'

'Lottie, you are crazy. But very romantic.'

She asked me whether I would stay with her for another three weeks. At the end of July, she had to travel to the south of France for a few days and then on to Geneva where she would remain with her husband for another year. I tried to imagine her husband. I pictured him as an older, elegant man dressed in a suit and tie and working in an important bank or insurance company or in an embassy.

'Do you have any children?' I felt a flash of guilt as soon as I'd let it out.

'No,' she said, lowering her head, as if the guilt had been passed on to her.

As if owning up to something, she added, 'I have never been able to conceive. It's as if my whole life I've never really been an adult. Like Peter Pan.'

I raised my hand and touched her face. She blushed a little. She placed her hand on mine.

'Three weeks,' I agreed.

I sent a text to my roommate, telling him not to worry if I wasn't around.

The days with Lottie were luxurious, like a holiday in the Caribbean or on a cruise. We spoke about a thousand different things and went all around the city visiting cafés and art galleries. Everything felt like it could come to an end at any moment.

One day I asked her about the paintings that were hanging in the staircase of her house. They were all of serious, slightly overweight men and painted in dark oils. Each had a small metal plaque beneath it bearing the surname Jones-Walker.

'Are they your family?' I asked.

'No, they are my husband's ancestors.'

They all looked alike and I guessed that the husband must look the same too, just in more modern clothes. I was able to guess from all the empty spaces around the house, on shelves, on nightstands and her dresser, that Lottie had decided to hide all the photos where her husband appeared.

In addition to being beautiful and fun, Lottie was generous. She always came back to the house with some kind of gift, often clothes of some kind, like a corduroy jacket, or pink Ralph Lauren trousers. Normally I would never have been seen dead in that kind of thing, but in Lottie's company they almost became a kind of costume.

Lottie was enrolled in an assortment of courses at the university, generally in the arts and humanities as far as I could tell.

One night in the garden she spoke of her husband, which until that moment she had generally managed to avoid.

'I asked my husband if he would read the story I had to analyse and the essay I wrote about it,' she said, pausing to take some tea. 'He's so busy he normally doesn't have any time to read. But he does look after me.'

'He's not much of a reader?' I asked with a kind of superior pleasure.

'Not really. He reads *The Times* and *The Telegraph*,

but that's a different kind of reading.' She paused with her tea held just in front of her, 'It made me very happy that he enjoyed the story. It probably wasn't a brilliant essay, academically speaking. I suppose it's not important anyway.' Her teacup remained suspended in the space in front of her, unmoving and elegant like the hour hand on a grandfather clock.

The last night there were tears. I guess she knew we would never see each other again and that these days had been a small luxury she could only allow herself once in a lifetime. Eventually, I began to forget Lottie, though at first I would still occasionally walk through her street and look up at her house. It had a melancholy vibe about it, the closed curtains in the upper windows transforming it into a blind and vulnerable entity.

Three winters passed. By then I had a job in John Lewis and was in a much better situation generally. Everything was much more stable anyway.

By pure coincidence one day, I walked past Daniel in Sloane Square. We both turned our heads and he decided to engage me, which I interpreted as a kind of apology. He told me about how James had eventually fired him too. How several Gourmet Food workers had been fired around that time.

'Since the bombs on the underground no one wants to have a party in the city centre anymore.'

I gave him the name of my boss and the very next week he was working with us as a security guard in the makeup section. I was now the manager in charge of the CCTV system which was boring but steady, paid the bills and even allowed me to put something away. All I had to do was file incident reports every now and again and manage the guys who monitored the security cameras.

One Sunday afternoon I saw Daniel on the monitor detaining a woman. I grabbed the controls off Peter, a blond kid from Manchester who worked the afternoon shift. I zoomed in.

I recognised the face but needed a few seconds. It was her. No doubt about it.

I ran downstairs to the makeup section to take charge of the situation and, hopefully, to help her out. It was busy and it wasn't easy getting to them. When I finally found them, Daniel had her by the arm.

'I'll take it from here. I know her.' Daniel looked at me with surprise, but let go of Lottie and left me to look after the situation. He carried away the Molton Skin Lotion pack she had stuffed into her bag.

I accompanied her to the entrance. She was much thinner than before. Her hair was longer and her eyes were a little swollen and dull.

'Recognise me?' I asked.

'No,' she replied faintly.

'What is your name?'

'They call me Lottie.'

I opened my wallet and gave her what I had, which she stuffed straight into her black plastic purse. I wanted to kiss her but instead I watched her fragile figure make its way into the dark, busy street and disappear. A gust of wind carried a scent of sandalwood and cinnamon.

Gunter Silva Passuni
Translated from Spanish by Dominic Zugai

Editors

Michael Kindellan
Emily-Rose Baker
Samraghni Bonnerjee
Eleanor Slater
Melanie Smiley

Holes in the road

The M1 is an asphalt lullaby, a concert of ambient noise that drags me into slumber as surely as it does towards my destination. It's strange how active the mind can be while half asleep in the back of a car; how the memories of similar journeys blur together or ping-pong back and forth in time, leaving me staring out at passing landscapes, half real and half remembered. I raced raindrops on the window as a child, and now I'm doing it again: tracing their hesitant progress down the glass, only for thoughts to distract me before the race is decided. How many times have I come this way, driving home through the dark?

I pay more attention to distant street lights than to the stars, travelling through a transposed cosmos, with its shifting constellations of headlights and cat's eyes. I drift toward Sheffield's heliopause in a homesick astronaut's hypersleep dream, but I always wake before the journey's end. In years past, it would end at the Tinsley cooling towers, their familiar silhouette an unspoken 'I'm home.' Now it ends when I note their absence.

I am trying to locate the city of my childhood; trying to determine how much of the Sheffield I remember is fiction and how much is simply gone like the towers. There are memories I know to be unreliable, like those of winding, shop-lined subterranean streets that could not possibly have existed. Yet, just as soon as I dismiss them, I discover a space where these hazy images start to fall into place.

The Hole in the Road isn't there anymore. In Castle Square, there is now a tram station over the site, surrounded by a circular patch of scar tissue. I can no longer walk the passageways of the Hole, or gaze up at the traffic circling above, so I may never know how much of my memory is accurate and how much is invented, replacing that which has slipped beyond its event horizon, or was buried within it when the council brought in the bulldozers. Still, those memories, invented or not, remain vivid. The chatter of crowds and chill of the air through underground passageways. Dimly lit shop windows and the shuffling homeless.

What happened to them, the crowds that circulated through those tunnels, the shopkeepers, the destitute and the drunk? When the black hole suffered its second collapse, maybe they were cast adrift, lost to the mercy of inertia. Or perhaps they were dragged deeper, spiralling towards the dark until the rubble blocked out the sun, victims of uncivil engineering.

It might be that I've met some of the Hole's refugees. The guy with the shabby beard, rambling back and forth in the city centre, cliché brown-paper covered bottle in hand who, when the mood took him, gave any woman unfortunate enough to be nearby a lecture on how to be a good mother. The man in the bar of the Showroom, who asked for directions to the station, only to spend the next twenty minutes telling me how much I reminded him of his best friend: a dead police officer.

Or perhaps not. Maybe, by stumbling across a few testimonies and images, I've merely found a convenient match for my memories or my fictions and transposed them along with the night sky.

On the M1, I awake to the city's approaching nebula.

Peter S Dorey

'The law of the fucking jungle'[1]: the objectification of women and animals in Michel Faber's *Under the skin* and Tobe Hooper's *The Texas chain saw massacre*

Exhibiting the patriarchal linguistic displacement through which women and nonhuman animals are objectified, Carol Adams' notion of the 'absent

1   Michel Faber, *Under the skin* (Edinburgh: Canongate, 2000), 35.
2   Carol Adams, *The sexual politics of meat: a feminist-vegetarian critical theory* (New York: Continuum, 2004), 51.
3   Karen Warren, 'The power and promise of ecological feminism', *Environmental Ethics* 12 (1990), 123.
4   Hilary Malatino, 'Carnophallogocentrism and *The sexual politics of meat*: review of the twentieth anniversary reissue of Carol J Adams' *The sexual politics of meat*', *Journal for Critical Animal Studies* 9, 3 (2011), 129.

referent', central to her work *The sexual politics of meat*, serves to exemplify the inextricable link between speciesism and gender inequality. Adams' feminist-vegetarian critical theory articulates that animals, like women, are made absent through gastronomic language that 'renames dead bodies before consumers participate in eating them': within this process, the slaughter of the dead animal is dissociated from the idea of meat.[2] Drawing upon the misogynistic animalisation and brutalisation of women inherent within the history of the horror film and its 'slasher' subgenre, I will apply Adams' structure to Hooper's *The Texas chain saw massacre* to expose how this shared female-animal 'logic of domination' converges literally in the cannibalistic procurement and consumption of Pam.[3] Complicating Adams' theory, however, an interrogation of protagonist Isserley, an extraterrestrial 'woman' who is paradoxically both sexual predator and sexualised prey in Faber's *Under the skin*, will demonstrate that 'woman' and 'animal' are not dichotomous states of being: Adams insists upon an 'essentialist variety of radical feminism' which fails to recognise the irreducible differences between these beings.[4] While Adams' theory offers a useful framework for tracing patterns of animal and female subjugation in Western culture then, it is the androcentric assumption inherent within Adams' theory, that woman and animal can be ontologised, that is responsible for their mutual oppressions.

Blurring the boundaries between woman and animal, Hooper insists upon the eroticised victimisation of women that has become 'synonymous with the

slasher film', in a physical representation of the mystification of meat inherent within Adams' theory.[5] For
Adams, the physical process of butchering an animal
is metaphorised verbally through language of
objectification and fragmentation, and it is precisely
this metaphor that is literalised in *The Texas chain saw
massacre*, through the slaughtering process of Pam.
On approaching the Texan family home of cannibals
'the Sawyers', Hooper invites his viewer to participate
in the voyeuristic male gaze of barely-clothed Pam:
the camera pans up her exposed body before zooming
out and stalking her from behind; the low-angle shot
transfixing predatorily on her naked flesh.[6] Drawing
attention to the meatiness of her form, this immediate
fetishisation of Pam's flesh as both sexual and edible,
coerces the viewer into assuming the place of the
masculinised omniscient narrator, perpetuating
the active male gaze which 'sees not the fragmented
flesh of dead animals but appetizing food'.[7] John
Berger, in his work *About looking*, asserts that 'animals
are always observed. The fact that they can observe
us has lost all significance'.[8] In this, Berger demonstrates the way in which animals, like women,
are repeatedly subjected to the oppressive virile gaze
enacted by Hooper, which regards them as meat
and denies them perspective. Stumbling into the lair
of her sadomasochistic torturer, Pam falls through
a door to find herself in a bed of decomposing animal
bones and bird feathers; the non-diegetic sound

5   Andrew Welsh, 'On the perils of living dangerously in the slasher horror film: gender differences in
    the association between sexual activity and survival', *Sex Roles* 62, 11 (2010), 732.
6   Tobe Hooper, *The Texas chain saw massacre*, ed. by Larry Carroll and Sallye Richardson
    (Vortex, 1974), 38–40.
7   Adams, *Sexual politics of meat*, 178.
8   John Berger, *About looking* (London: Bloomsbury, 2009), 14.
9   Hooper.
10 Carol Adams, *Animals and women: feminist theoretical explanations*, ed. by Carol Adams
    and Josephine Donovan (Durham and London: Duke University Press, 1995), 12.

of a chicken clucking infiltrating the scene. Before
looking up from the floor to reveal the skeletal remains of both humans and animals (now transformed
into furniture), Hooper juxtaposes close-up shots
of Pam's nauseated expression with that of a caged
chicken hanging from the ceiling.[9] The significance
of the chicken, intensified by its clucking, the
feathers and its constant intercuts, is made unavoid-
able as the camera shot zooms in and its entrapped
form fills the frame, serving as a condemning
reminder of the incessant dissociative language that
effaces the reality of slaughter: in forcing images of
skeleton, woman and animal into proximity, Hooper
emphasises the linkage between live animal and
dead corpse. Likewise, the interspersed close-ups
of Pam's face in this sequence demonstrate the way
in which women are implicated in this dissociative
process: women are objectified sexually through
absenting language of consumption. The way this
linguistic relationship between woman and meat
manifests in patriarchal culture is examined by
Alleen Pace Nilsen, who articulates how chickens
have become intrinsic signifiers for the various stages
of female livelihood: 'a young girl is a *chick*. [...]
Eventually she has her *brood*, begins to *henpeck* her
husband, and finally turns into an *old biddy*.'[10]
In this, Nilsen depicts the sexist absenting of women
integral to the absent referent, and the fact that
the chicken sharing the room with Pam in the film
is not the source of the clucking when she enters
the scene, indicates that this making-absent is
universal: the sound denotes that of the collective
animal who is, like the chicken in the room, imprisoned, de-feathered or skinned, murdered and

renamed. Hooper's recurrent motif of the entrapped chicken also provides an explicit critique of the intensification of industrialised animal farming from the nineteen-sixties, particularly within the predominantly agricultural state of Texas. In this way, the chicken's barred cage, barely large enough to contain it and hung up in physical objectification, not only is illustrative of its entrapment within this linguistic system of oppression, but of Hooper's contempt for such maltreatment also.

Forcing Pam and viewer alike to confront the murder and suffering of animals, Hooper continues his feminist-vegetarian strand through the image of Pam-as-animal, making present the transmuted fate of the animal within the concept of meat. Failing to escape the Sawyers' home, Pam is carried by Leatherface into a processing room; the camera shifting in perspective to observe the scene from behind a bloody meat hook, bringing slaughter, as that which is obscured in the absent referent, to the forefront.[11] Zooming out to reveal the bloody reality of animal slaughter, Hooper's camera jumps again to reveal the slaughterhouse apparatus in full: blood splatters the walls, evoking the murder of those before Pam. Finally, after lifting Pam onto the meat hook, Leatherface tosses a fork into the sink and starts his chainsaw, the camera honing in on the bucket collecting her blood before panning

11 Hooper.
12 Ibid.
13 Carol J Clover, 'Her body, himself: gender in the slasher film', *Representations* 20 (1987), 198.
14 Cary Wolfe, 'Subject to sacrifice: ideology, psychoanalysis, and the discourse of species in Jonathan Demme's *The silence of the lambs*', *animal rites: American culture, the discourse of species and posthumanist theory* (London: University of Chicago Press, 2003), 100.
15 Carol Adams, *Neither man nor beast: feminism and the defence of animals* (New York: Continuum, 1995), 41.
16 Adams, *Sexual politics of meat*, 58.

up her writhing body.[12] Refusing to censor the reality
of the slaughter process this way, Hooper reverses
the absent referent, making explicit the cruel hanging of animals, sometimes still conscious and left
to die in severe distress. In her essay 'Gender in the
slasher film', Carol J. Clover states that 'the slasher
evinces a fascination with flesh or meat itself as
that which is hidden from view', and it is the con-
cealment of meat as emblematic of the workings
of the absent referent, that Hooper works to expose
throughout the film.[13] The indifference with which
Leatherface impales Pam on the hook before walking away, evident within the juxtaposed shots of
her tormented cries and Leatherface's fork, reflects
the ignorance inherent within the absent referent
process: as consumers of the 'meat' of the animal
Pam substitutes, we dissociate from the animal
and deny acknowledgement of its painful death to
extricate moral obligation for their murder. As
Derrida states, 'carnivorous sacrifice is essential to
the structure of subjectivity' and so shapes the
'basis of our culture and law', and this law is made
tangible in the image of Pam as sexualised meat:[14]
Pam conforms to Adams' notion that 'the object's
own intrinsic subjectivity is irrelevant'.[15] While Pam
is objectified as a piece of meat in the most extreme
sense, she is equally made into a sexual object:
penetrated by the phallic hook, she is held up on
display to be looked at, rendered helpless. In this
sexual objectification, Pam undergoes a metaphori-
cal consumption, identified by Adams as 'the
fulfilment of oppression, the annihilation of will,
of separate identity'.[16] Like the imprisoned chicken,
Pam is physically restrained at the mercy of her

killer and at the expense of her subjectivity, the close-up shots of her gasping face not only depicting her pain and vulnerability but, disturbingly, resembling orgasmic release. In this way, the secretion of blood trickling down her bare legs into the bucket beneath not only is expressive of the way in which the blood of animals is left to drain from their bodies, but also emulates a post-intercoursal state, particularly in parallel with Pam's agonised convulsions.[17] This sexualised torturing of Pam, objectifying her as both edible and sexual, is symptomatic of the slasher's propagation of prolonged and extreme graphic violence against women: the males in the film are murdered quickly and without sustained suffering, while the females endure the most sadistic deaths. Such ultimate interpenetration of butchering and sexual violence then exerts the 'extremely specific, assaultive ways in which "meat" is used to refer to women' through language.[18]

In adherence with the basic premise of Adams' theory, that women and nonhuman animals are indeed objectified through patriarchal language displacement, Faber exposes the misogynistic objectification of Isserley's body through the lens of her male hitchhikers in the first half of *Under the skin*. Initially establishing a reversed animal-human binary, Faber facilitates a linguistic inversion with which new meaning is ascribed to the human; intensively farmed 'vodsels' taking the place of animals. Without exception, Isserley's breasts are appraised by every vodsel

17 Hooper, *The Texas chainsaw massacre.*
18 Adams, 70.
19 Faber, 35.
20 Ibid.
21 Ibid., 178.

who enters her car, expressing her body in terms of its utility as an object for sexual consumption: 'Her tits would dangle between his legs. He'd give them a bit of a squeeze if she did a good job. She'd do her best, he could tell. Breathing hard already she was, like a bitch in heat'.[19] Before raping Isserley, this hitcher ontologises her solely as an instrument, valuable only as a means to sexual gratification. The use of 'tits' reduces Isserley to an object and negates her selfhood, while in referring to her as a 'bitch' he both elicits the kind of abusive language used against women and pertains to Isserley as equally-brutalised animal. This 'law' of the jungle then, the 'force of nature' authorising the hitcher to objectify Isserley without moral consideration, discerns the patriarchal law with which women and animals are rendered absent as subjects.[20] Not only is Isserley figuratively dismembered this way, but the gruesome reality of her body modification, trans-forming her from human (animal) to vodsel (woman), signifies her physical mutilation. Modelled on a glamour model from a pornographic magazine, Isserley is disfigured so that she can be objectified by male vodsels and lure them into her predatory snare. Akin to the physical dismemberment of ani-mals in the farming industry, Isserley endures the removal of her tail and sixth finger, the insertion of a metal rod in her spine, and the replacement of her teats: 'Her real teats, budding naturally from her abdomen, had been surgically removed [...] The surgeons had used pictures from a magazine sent by Esswis as a guide'.[21] Through the painful destruc-tion of Isserley's former anatomy and subsequent disintegration of her identity, Faber simulates the butchering of animals eclipsed in the linguistic invention and consumption of 'meat'. Bringing Isserley's now 'puffy' breasts into focus, Faber emphasises the incongruence between her former teats, as emblems of fertility, and her now bulging 'tumours'.[22] The fact that Isserley's breasts are so painfully and artificially inflated serves to condemn the patriarchal fetishisation of women's bodies, their synthetic quality rendering them empty signifiers, reduced to objects for sexual gratification: her breasts, which have no biological function, signify both her sexual and reproductive marginalisation. This total marginalisation of Isserley is further realised as we learn of her removed genitals, which deny her fulfilment of instinctual sexual compulsions and an inherent procreative purpose: 'Only when she realised that some of her fingers had strayed between her legs, searching blindly for what was no longer to be found there, did she come back to her senses and rinse herself with businesslike efficiency.'[23] The disparity between Isserley's 'blind' attempt to retrieve her sexuality and the 'business-like efficiency' with which she manages the trauma of her marginalisation emphasises her irreversible transition into object status: stripped of humanity, she is the literal embodiment of male fantasy, surgically constructed to be objectified by another male species. Drawing a comparison between Isserley and Medusa, Ara Osterweil states that while

22 Ibid., 177.
23 Ibid., 148.
24 Ara Osterweil, '*Under the skin:* the perils of becoming female', *Female Quarterly* 67, 4 (2014), 48.
25 Wolfe, 'Subject to sacrifice', 46.
26 Adams, *Sexual politics of meat*, 60.
27 Faber, 35.
28 Sarah Dillon, '"It's a question of words, therefore": becoming animal in Michel Faber's *Under the skin*', *Science Fiction Studies* 38 No. 1 (2011), 151.

Isserley is predator in *Under the skin*, like Medusa,
her power is 'stolen and used to annihilate her'.[24]
Corresponding with Freud's notion that 'anatomy
is destiny' then, this annihilation of Isserley's
subjectivity is made inevitable within the novel
by the male vodsels who view her as inherently usable
for sex.[25]

Reproducing this predatory male gaze onto her
hitchers however, the male vodsels become
the recipient of *Isserley's* sexual objectification in a
subversion of conventional patriarchal power
relations, exposing the internal workings of the
absent referent. From the novel's sexualised opening,
Isserley replicates the dominant patriarchal gaze
which views 'the sexually desired object as consum-
able':[26] 'She was looking for big muscles: a hunk
on legs. Puny, scrawny specimens were of no use to
her'.[27] Evoking sexual and carnivorous appetites
through Isserley's explicit language of objectification,
Faber evinces the linkage between sex and violence
symptomatic of the absent referent. This imbrication
of the discourse of predation and seduction, of
the erotic and the predatory, verbally converges the
consumption of sex and that of meat, absenting
the vodsels from their living bodies. As the unantici-
pated female source of such a gaze, Dillon writes
that we 'interpret Isserley's intentions towards her
targets as sexual, rather than sinister', yet Faber
exploits and redirects this attention upon sexuality
toward the vodsels as an edible species, making
blatant that she is concerned only with males of
a particular, meaty, calibre.[28] That said, Faber's use
of 'hunk' refers not only to the muscular body

of a sexually attractive man, but to an actual piece of meat, just as Isserley's disinterest in 'Puny, scrawny specimens' not only implies a sexual desire for a man who is physically well-endowed, but according to zoological terminology, is used to appraise the body of the animal. In this, Faber depicts the language displacement that, while functioning through the objectification of male vodsels here, is enacted against women and animals. Adams contends that animals are 'rendered being-less [...] by innocuous phrases such as "food-producing unit"', and Faber's detailing of 'vodissin', which is 'neatly parcelled into portions, swathed in transparent viscose, packed into plastic pallets' deploys such phrases to exemplify this displacement.[29] Here, Faber addresses meat as a separate entity to the living vodsels themselves, substituting the dead vodsel for mystified vodissin, while references to synthetic materials 'viscose' and 'plastic' demonstrate the laboured displacement process, mirroring that of transforming animals into edible commodities, the use of 'swathed' marking an attempt to make meat unrecognisable. The incessancy of Faber's plosive alliteration likewise exposes the perpetual ignorance with which we package dead animals without daring to conceive of their deaths. Corresponding with Adams' claim that 'we opt for less disquieting referent points not only by changing names from animals to meat, but by cooking, seasoning, and covering the animals with sauces, disguising their original nature'

29 Adams, *Sexual politics of meat*, 27.
30 Ibid., 59.
31 Faber, 171.
32 Ibid., 174.
33 Cary Wolfe, *Zoontologies: the question of the animal*
      (Minneapolis: University of Minnesota Press, 2003), xvi.
34 Dillon, 'It's a question of words, therefore', 146.

then, demonstrates that by wrapping the meat up, we conceal the ugly truth of its death, absenting the blood and torture of the slaughter made explicit by Hooper.[30]

However, Faber problematizes Adams' structure in the latter half of his novel, through the gradual breaking down of speciesist assumptions which determine Isserley's selfhood, as that which is separate from the vodsels she hunts. After watching, 'disturbed', as a desperate vodsel engraves 'M E R C Y' into the soil of his pen, Isserley becomes obsessed with exerting herself in opposition with the vodsels to prevent the ethical problematics of being more closely associated with their species than she realised.[31] In an attempt to convince herself of their precarious division, she protests that vodsels 'couldn't do any of the things that really defined a human being. They couldn't siuwil, they couldn't menishtil, they had no concept of slan'.[32] Condemning the 'no language, no subjectivity' formula identified by Wolfe, Faber establishes the arbitrary nature of Isserley's species exceptionalism, via the importance she places upon the possession of fictional concepts.[33] In justifying her superiority through a mastery of a language rendered incomprehensible to the reader then, Isserley inadvertently violates this linguistic barrier she so desperately erects. Referring to the work of Deleuze and Guattari, Dillon insists that in this frenzied attempt to define herself in opposition with vodsels, Isserley undergoes a 'becoming-animal' transformation so that her identity is defined 'in relationality with the other and not in opposition to it'.[34] This becoming-animal through language marks the dismantling of Isserley's humanness, and determines her eventual suicide, as she realises she no longer fits within her self-ontologised view of herself as 'human' or, indeed, 'woman'. That said, following her car accident at the close of the novel, Isserley refers to the female vodsel who comes to her aid as 'the other woman', who wraps her up 'in the anorak, gently tucking it around her shoulders'.[35] Here, Isserley overtly evidences her becoming-animal, as she not only affords this female vodsel human status in acknowledgement of her personhood, but in bearing the anorak used previously to disguise incapacitated hitchers, aligns herself with those vodsels she hunted. Implicit in Adams' methodology is a prototyped model of woman, a 'categorically conceived and universalized woman', yet through Isserley's becoming-animal Faber articulates that woman and vodsel, like human and nonhuman animal, are not dichotomous conditions.[36] As Malatino writes, the absent referent works 'within a logic of presence and absence, a dialectic of full being and mere matter that ties a categorically conceived and universalized 'woman' to the non-human animal'.[37] In other words, it is precisely because woman and animal are conceived of as general singulars that they are oppressed in Western culture. As Judith Butler writes, 'it seems crucial to resist the model of power that would set up racism and misogyny and homophobia as parallel or analogous relations' because such a model 'delays

35 Faber, 294–5.
36 Malatino, 'Review of *The sexual politics of meat*', 133.
37 Ibid., 133.
38 Judith Butler, quoted in 'Subject to sacrifice', 99.
39 Jacques Derrida, 'Eating well', *Points…interviews, 1974–1994*, ed. Elisabeth Weber
     (Standford: Stanford University Press, 1995), 285.
40 Ibid., 285.

the important work of thinking through the ways in which these vectors of power require and deploy each other for the purpose of their own articulation'.[38] Speciesism, like sexism, can be assimilated neither to notions of 'the woman' nor of 'the animal', as this understanding of being is reductive: in order to apprehend and respond to the objectification of woman and animal, any theory necessarily has to problematize the division between these subjects.

Adams' formula, then, is ultimately one of simplicity. As demonstrated through Hooper's slasher and the beginnings of Faber's discourse of species, woman and animal equally succumb to a similar patriarchal objectification through language. Yet, as Faber validates through Isserley's inevitable suicide, this acknowledgement is not enough to radically alter the othering of woman and animal, because it refuses to challenge the ontological assumptions which inherently deny these beings' subjectivity. Prescribing a reconstitution of the language underpinning the 'binary opposition between the human and the infra-human' in his interview 'Eating Well', Derrida states: 'These possibilities or necessities, without which there would be no language, are *themselves not only human.*'[39] In order for animals, like women, to be conceived of as subjects then, we must re-inscribe language as Faber does in *Under the skin*: rather than assigning woman and animal stable ontologies, we must consider 'scientific knowledge about the complexity of "animal languages"' to avert their dual subjugations.[40]

Emily-Rose Baker

Finding closure above the clouds

I did not learn of my grandad's passing until three days after it had happened. It was my own fault I guess, setting off to remote places knowing he was not in the best condition. A mix of guilt and regret were the first things I felt; then came the sadness and the thought that I could have been there. I could have visited and seen him once more, but at the time the idea of going on a hike around Mont Blanc seemed far more exciting than spending a couple of days with my grandparents in Spain.

I wrote him a letter two days before leaving, telling him that I knew we would be doing this trip together if he was my age. I said I could not wait to be back and recount to him my adventures on the trail and show him all the pictures. I wanted to show him

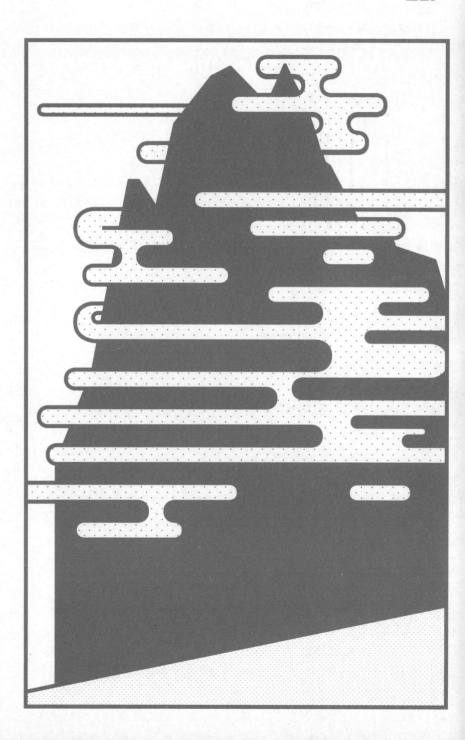

who I have become and what I am capable of now.
And so I set off on a ten-day hike around the highest
mountain in Western Europe, carrying everything
I would need during the 170 km trek in a backpack.
Across France, Italy and Switzerland, I hiked up wild
mountains, crossed peaceful prairies, walked through
green valleys and slept before ageless glaciers.

I had never hiked for so long before, let alone planned
a trip of such grand scale or camped at a different
spot every night. Trying to picture the full distance
your feet have taken you is really hard to process. To
look into the horizon and clearly see the point where
you came from that morning, far, far away. To know
that you have crossed countries by no other means
than your legs—no cars, buses or trains required...

On the first day, as the hours went by and I was still
going uphill, I did wonder why on earth I was there,
putting myself in so much discomfort and pain.
My legs hurt from carrying a big backpack for so long,
I sweated all day and the trail was pretty challenging—
but it was so beautiful. The views kept me in awe
and the fact that it comes completely down to you,
and you alone, to be standing in that exact spot,
is truly mind-blowing.

It is not only about the views though, there is a
special aspect in the walking itself. Trekking is so
different from everyday life, when you can just
put off what you have to do for an uncertain amount
of time. Or sometimes you are working, but it
doesn't feel like anything is being achieved. When
it comes to a long trail there is no opportunity to

procrastinate and it is beautiful. Whilst hiking
I never stood in the exact same spot, and even if I did
not reach my destination, I would still be so far off
the point where I was standing that morning, always
moving forward.

There was a certain conflicting sense of progress on
this route—every step takes you further from the
start point, but as you walk away and move forwards
you also come closer to the beginning of the trail
again. The best way I can try to explain it is like drawing a circle, looking for closure, and coming back
to the beginning.

I found my grandad again in a warm Italian sunset.
My emotions were up and down, as if their only duty
was to echo the pattern of the path I was walking
on. Slowly it felt like I was back in Spain, watching
the sun go down from the terrace, with him by
my side cracking almonds open. For a second I could
even hear the sound the shells made as they broke;
then I was back in Italy, certain that I had been next
to him on that mild summer evening.

I know my being there would not have changed
the outcome of things, but I still wish I could have
sat next to him and watched the moon rise into
the night sky together one last time. I did not expect
my journey to be an emotional one so much as a
physical one when I set off, but it turned out to be
so. I may not have been in Spain with him, but in
a sense he was trekking with me.

Carolina Kyllmann

Community, commonality and creativity: social innovation and education

During a time when the national media seems full of reports of anger, fear and tectonic shifts in macro level discourse, it is timely to remember that 'top

1   *Leeds City Council,* 18 November 2016, www.leeds.gov.uk.
2   *Visit Leeds,* 18 November 2016, www.visitleeds.co.uk.
3   *Lonely Planet Guide,* 18 November 2016, www.lonelyplanet.com.

down' policy is not the only factor that determines our existence and experiences. Based in Leeds, I am fortunate to work with a range of social initiatives that seek to change the world from a grassroots, 'bottom up' perspective, and from my position I see optimism, impact and proactive passion.

According to Leeds City Council, 'Leeds is the UK's fastest growing city with a £56 billion economy, a combined population of 3 million and a workforce of 1.5 million', and they forecast that in the coming ten years the regional economy will 'grow by 25%'.[1] According to the Visit Leeds website, 'Leeds is a delight to explore and ripe for discovery. A compact and vibrant city centre, attracting visitors for its world class live music, sport, cultural heritage, shopping and fabulous food and drink'.[2] As a Leeds resident I do not dispute this, and I hope that the 26 million day visitors attracted to the 'Knightsbridge of the North'[3] find their expectations met. However, this glossy portrayal does little to illuminate the grit that underpins the grass roots, and jack boots, associated with the region. For that I now turn to four people in Leeds that are changing the not-so-palatable experiences that surround them.

Adam Smith was so appalled at the amount of food wasted across the globe, he returned to his native Leeds to launch The Real Junk Food Project. Knowing that approximately one third of all food produced ends up in landfill, for the past four years, Adam has ensured he has done all he can to prevent edible food being wasted. In doing so he has put into practice an alternative economic model that centres

on community, sustaining the environment and
challenging the destructive nature of disposable
consumerism. Initially Adam opened a pay-as-you-
feel café in Armley, where food that would otherwise
have been wasted was cooked and served by vol-
unteers and offered to the local community. Those
that ate paid in whatever way they could; some
with money, others with their time and labour.
Here the inclusive diners were not means-tested,
as the mission to eradicate unnecessary waste can
be championed by individuals from every facet
of society, and in this community the ambassadors
eat together. The success of this venture led to the
organic development of an international network
of 110 cafes. Agreements with a range of super-
markets means that unsold food can be collected
and used if viable. The network has so far saved over
107,000 tons of food from waste, and has delivered
more than 90,000 meals to over 60,000 people.
Not content with one surplus-saving model, Adam
has now opened a pay-as-you-feel supermarket.
Although similar surplus-supermarket models
are opening in other parts of the world, this is the
first in England, and again it is pioneered in
Leeds. From a warehouse in Pudsey, the take-what-
you-want and pay-as-you-feel offer is made to
those who are willing to use this service to help
eliminate waste.

Whilst eliminating waste is a priority for this organi-
sation, there is no doubt that a secondary benefit
is the increased availability of cheaper food for local
low income residents who may be struggling in
the current economic climate. But what happens

if you live in an area of Leeds that has been designated a 'food desert', where there are no shops, no super-markets and few local amenities? Despite the 'over-all' descriptions provided at the beginning of this piece, Leeds does contain communities that would struggle to see themselves reflected accurately in them. However, within some of the most challenging environments, social innovation, creative solutions and personal drive are empowering and inspiring change.

Richmond Hill Primary School is based in the Hunslet area of Leeds, and its catchment is such that pupil premium funding is used to support the development of many of the children in its care. Recognising the 'food desert' surrounding the school and acknowledging that children were coming to school hungry, the Head Teacher, Nathan Atkinson, decided that the physical needs of his pupils required addressing before academic development could effectively take place. To combat this, he liaised with The Real Junk Food Project and sourced surplus food to continuously provide a no-cost breakfast for each of the 600 pupils at the school. This had a positive effect on children's behaviour, concentration levels and ultimately has raised the educational attainment across the school. Mr Atkinson furthered this achievement through the creation of a community pay-as-you-feel café within the school grounds, and invited the local residents to use it as a recreational space. In doing so, he has created an inviting space where children, parents and families can communicate positively. The café can be accessed by anyone in the community, and is open throughout the year (for security reasons access to this facility does not provide access to the teaching spaces within the school).

Despite providing breakfast for hundreds of pupils and running the community café, there is still more surplus food to be disposed of than these ventures can handle. One consequence is that Richmond Hill provides a daily 'Market Stall' at the front of the school, with an Honesty Box to collect the pay-as-you-feel contributions. The success of this venture, and a desire to educate others, resulted in Fuel for School being developed out of a partnership between The Real Junk Food Project and Richmond Hill Primary School. This initiative has three key objectives:

— to remove hunger as a barrier to learning
— to highlight the importance of nutrition, well-being and the associated benefits to learning
— to highlight the vast amounts of edible wasted food across our local and wider communities.

Fuel for School is currently working with over 35 primary schools in the Leeds area, and twice a week delivers surplus food to them. The schools themselves determine the most productive way to use the food whether it be breakfast club activities, used as ingredients for cooking classes, or presented on a market stall within the school grounds. Service level agreements ensure that each school is visited by Fred the Fox (the official mascot of Fuel for School who embodies the values Feed, Recycle, Educate, Dine), and each school is provided with a range of educational resources designed to improve well-being. The demand for this has increased, and Fuel for School is about to begin exciting ventures with the secondary schools and universities in the area.

Recently Kevin Mackay from the Fuel for School project was invited by Professor Damien Page Dean of the Carnegie School of Education, Leeds Beckett University, to meet with students studying on the BA Education Studies programme. The visit marked the beginning of a series of collaborations, where students and staff are involved in the design and delivery of a number of educational resources and activities to support the Fuel for School project. Kevin described the mission of each of the projects presented above, and extended an invitation for student involvement. The issues raised clearly resonated with the students, who were enthusiastic to participate in such ventures.

As I observed at the beginning of this article, Leeds is a beautiful and vibrant city. It has a rich heritage and a relatively buoyant economy. However, the real wealth is in the people: their passion, their resilience, their creativity and their sheer determination. Some places will never be cited on the 'must see' lists of Leeds, but the value of these places and the people who occupy them contribute significantly to the culture and future of the city. As a Loiner I am proud to be part of a community that embraces difference, extends friendship and works together to enhance the well-being of all.

Anne Temple Clothier

Untitled
(World is at a turning point)

I dare you!

Get ahead in the race

Getting the job done.

The lives of young people are changing and dynamic.

Whether we do it matters: Nothing happens unless you take the first step. We take the initiative to change the game.

Visit the portal today

The world is at a turning point.

A once-in-a-generation chance to change the direction of our nation for good.

Initiatives to boost the future livings standards of younger people are pulled together in today's productivity plan.

But if you believe you're a citizen of the world, you're a citizen of nowhere.

Every product   works together,

our digital evidence management   system

integrates

bringing it to law   seamlessly   pushing the boundaries

breakdown   **ARE YOU ALWAYS**
the coming   exciting new   **RUNNING OUT OF TIME?**
                                       You can find bulk pricing by

decision-making

motivations   values   knowledge

and quiet resolve. A country of decency, fairness and quiet resolve. A country of decency,

fairness and qui   **We're all Conservatives here**   fairness and quiet resolve. A country of decer   country of decency, fairness and quiet resolve. A country of decency, and quiet resolve. A country of decency,   and quiet resolve. A country of decency, fairness and quiet resolve. A country of decency, fairness and quiet resolve. A country of decency, fairness and quiet resolve. A country of decency, fairness and qu   fairness and quiet resolve. A country of dece   **we're coming after you.**   country of decency, fairness and quiet resolv   nd quiet resolve. v A country

of decency, fairness and quiet resolve. A country of decency, fairness and quiet resolve. A country of decency, fairness and quiet resolve. A country of decency, fairness and quiet resolve. A country of decency, fairness and quiet resolve. A country of decency, fairness and quiet resolve. A country of decency, fairness and quiet resolve. A country of decency, fairness and quiet resolve. A country of decency, fairness and quiet resolve. A country of decency, fairness and quiet resolve. A country of decency, fairness and quiet resolve. A country of decency, fairness and quiet resolve. A country of decency, fairness and quiet resolve. A country of decency, fairness and quiet resolve. A country of decency, fairness and quiet resolve. A country of decency, fairness and quiet resolve. A country of decency, fairness and quiet resolve. A country of decency, fairness and quiet resolve. vvv A country of decency, fairness and quiet resolve. A country of decency, fairness and quiet resolve. A country of decency, fairness and quiet resolve. A country of decency, fairness and quiet resolve. A country of decency, fairness and quiet resolve. A country of decency, fairness and quiet resolve. A country of decency, fairness and quiet resolve. A country of decency, fairness and quiet resolve. A country of decency, fairness and quiet resolve. vv A country of decency, fairness and quiet resolve. A country of decency, fairness and quiet resolve. A country of decency, fairness and quiet resolve. A country of decency, fairness and quiet resolve. A country of decency, fairness and quiet resolve. A country of decency, fairness and quiet resolve. A country of decency, fairness and quiet

The Radical Theory Collective

On genre

Although Huxley's *Brave new world* and Shakespeare's *Romeo and Juliet* were written centuries apart, these texts employ generic conventions of tragedy relevant to both a Renaissance and a modern context. This essay will first explore the generic classification of these two texts: *Brave new world* is typically classified as a dystopia, yet given that dystopia and tragedy share many similar generic traits, Francesco Muzzioli's stance that 'We could see dystopia as the contemporary form of tragedy', enables a comparison of both works.[1] After defining dystopia and drawing comparisons between this genre and tragedy, this essay will explore *Romeo and Juliet* and *Brave new world* through the lens of Susan Synder's definition of tragedy: 'The tragic world is governed by inevitability, and its highest value is personal integrity', and will determine that inevitability and personal integrity are key to both texts.[2] When applying Synder's definition of tragedy to these works, it becomes apparent that the inevitability stems from the protagonists' inability to

1 Umberto Rosso, 'Dystopia or disaster?', *Science Fiction Studies* 35, 2 (2008), 334.
2 Susan Snyder, 'Romeo and Juliet: comedy into tragedy', *Essays in Criticism* 10, 4 (1970), 391.

3 Gregory Claeys, 'News from somewhere: enhanced sociability and the composite definition of utopia and dystopia', *History* 98, 330 (2013), 170.

escape from the structures of power that inhabit their world. In *Romeo and Juliet* this manifests itself primarily as the institution of patriarchal power, which controls how society functions and therefore dictates the rights of Romeo and Juliet. *Brave new world* is dominated by a futuristic system of dictatorship that rules virtually every aspect of human life. Whilst the structures of these societies may be fundamentally different given the differing historical contexts of the works, they both serve to impose laws on a society which the protagonists attempt to defy. Ultimately, the tragedy of both *Romeo and Juliet* and *Brave new world* is inevitable as a result of the protagonists' attempts to maintain their personal integrity by defying a power structure they are unable to overcome.

In order to compare *Romeo and Juliet*, a Shakespearean tragedy, with *Brave new world*, one must first endeavour to define Huxley's novel as a tragedy, which poses a challenge as *Brave new world* is universally classified as a dystopia. Yet through an analysis of the generic traits of both dystopia and tragedy, it is clear that the two are intrinsically linked; in essence, dystopia is rooted in tragedy. In his discourse concerning the definitions of utopia and dystopia, Gregory Claeys argues that, in terms of fiction, dystopia is epitomised by 'societies where human volition has been superseded or eroded by an authoritative imposition of control'.[3] This sense of a lack of individuality as a result of a dominating society runs throughout his discourse, suggesting that these are key to understanding dystopia as a genre. Claeys writes that dystopian societies value 'the privileging of conformity over dissent, and of the group over the individual',[4] and that 'dystopia evidences [...] the horrific nature of enforced communalism of the communist type, with its crushing loss of subjective individual identity'.[5] Similar ideas of individuality and the importance of powerful institutions are apparent in Hegelian discourse on tragedy. Hegel believed that 'to genuine *tragic* action it is essential that the principal of *individual* freedom and independence, or at least that of self-determination [...] have been aroused',[6] and that 'the essence of tragedy is conflict', more specifically 'a conflict between legitimate rights and institutions'.[7] Therefore for Hegel, tragedy arises when two opposing yet equally just forces—the force of the social and the force of the individual—come into conflict. Although the idea of a dystopian power being 'just' may seem distorted, Claeys concedes that dystopia 'can in certain circumstances be a deliberate strategy for social improvement', and so it is evident that modern theories of tragedy encompass similar generic characteristics to those present in dystopia.[8] Synder's interpretation of tragedy, too, considers this conflict between the individual and society. She explains that 'in the tragic world law is inherent: imposed by the individual's own nature, it may direct him to a conflict with the larger patterns of law inherent in his universe'.[9] This essay will therefore consider the role of the individual within the context of a society they oppose as a significant element of tragedy.

4 Ibid., 166.
5 Ibid., 172.
6 Raymond Williams, *Modern tragedy* (London: Chatto & Windus, 1966), 33.
7 Robert R Williams, *Tragedy, recognition and the death of God* (Oxford: Oxford University Press, 2013), 120.
8 Claeys, 163.
9 Snyder, 391.

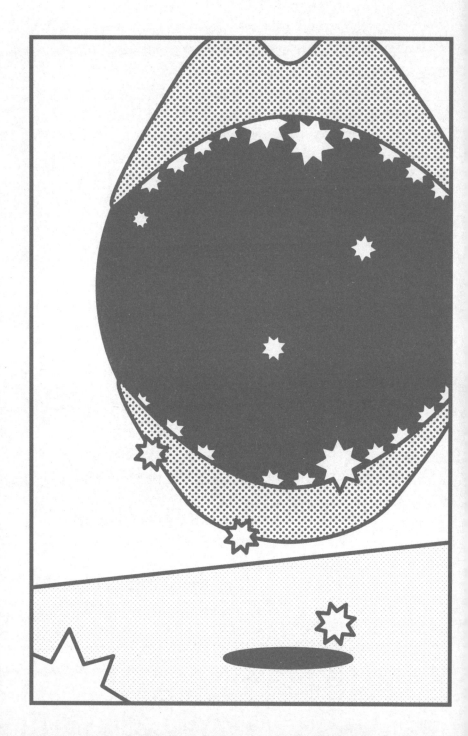

However, this understanding of tragedy does not withdraw from Synder's focus on inevitability and personal integrity as fundamental traits of tragedy. Personal integrity essentially denotes an individual's persistence in continuing to act in a way they consider to be moral or right, regardless of the punishment or suffering they receive as a result. If personal integrity is the struggle of an individual against an outside force, then the emphasis on the fight for individuality in both Claeys and Hegel's exploration of dystopia and tragedy respectively is simply another way of expressing this concept of personal integrity. Furthermore, both Hegel and Claeys seem to express a sense of inevitability in their analysis. In the process of defining Dystopia, Claeys notes that 'dystopia represents a loss of control, often finally and absolutely'.[10] These adverbs evoke a sense of inevitability, suggesting that these dystopian governments cannot be successfully overthrown. The concept of inevitability is more evident in Hegel's idea of tragedy, as he argues that the conflict between the individual and the state inevitably results in tragic resolution, which is most commonly the fall of the tragic hero: 'the hero is destroyed by the very powers s/he refuses to recognise'.[11] Hence, tragedy will subsequently be defined through the lens of Synder, Claeys, and Hegel's discourses, with particular emphasis on the individual's attempt to maintain their personal integrity during conflict with society, and the inevitability of a tragic outcome for the protagonist as a result of this conflict.

10   Claeys, 170.
11   Williams, *Tragedy*, 120.
12   William C Carroll, '"We were born to die": Romeo and Juliet', *Comparative Drama*, 15, 1 (1981), 57.

13   William Shakespeare, 'Romeo and Juliet', *The complete works of Shakespeare*, ed. Jonathan Bate and Eric Rasmussen (Hampshire: Macmillan, 2007), 1696.
14   Ibid., 1709.

Brave new world and *Romeo and Juliet* can be defined as tragedies through this interpretation, as both tragic worlds are governed by institutions that dictate how society functions. In *Romeo and Juliet*, this is the patriarchal society which controls both familial power and the institution of marriage. Carroll notes that the lovers 'are almost always entangled in family webs [and] surrounded by well-meaning but interfering authority figures', thus marking the family feud as the main obstacle that the lovers face.[12] Juliet urges Romeo to break with his familial ties, as abandoning his identity as a Montague would enable their love to flourish without being subject to the constraints of the feud: 'deny thy father and refuse thy name'.[13] Yet as the play progresses it is clear that neither of the lovers can escape their familial bonds. In Act Three, Scene One, Romeo maintains his personal integrity by staying true to his own moral compass and refusing to fight Tybalt. In essence, his love of Juliet supercedes his desire to uphold his family's honour, which angers Mercutio who condemns his 'dishonourable, vile submission'.[14] However, when Romeo realises that his attempt to prevent the fight results in Mercutio's fatal wound, he sacrifices his personal desires in order to avenge the death of Mercutio. Romeo's personal integrity and the needs of the patriarchal order coincide here, but only fleetingly, as this action creates more obstacles that the lovers must overcome. Thus, when Romeo submits to the demands of the patriarchy, his own desire to unite with Juliet becomes an even harder goal to reach. For Juliet, the main source of oppression is that of her proposed marriage to Paris, which her father insists upon: 'she will be ruled in all respects by me'; 'she shall be married'.[15] Capulet speaks bluntly, demonstrating his absolute authority over Juliet as her father. Yet Juliet declares: 'I will not marry yet', demonstrating her defiance against the system of patriarchy that oppresses her individual desire.[16] It is important to note that her father's steadfast resolve results in her need to fake her own death, demonstrating the extreme lengths one must go to in order to defy the patriarchal institution of marriage. Despite Romeo and Juliet's efforts to resist societal pressure, the oppressive patriarchal society influences and drives their actions: the lovers are constantly trying to overcome the obstacles that society puts in their path, but ultimately they cannot be together *and* still be accepted by the patriarchal order.

The repression of the individual and personal integrity is also key to *Brave new world*. In the first section of the novel, Bernard represents the individual's struggle in an unaccepting oppressive society. Huxley employs the lexis of isolation when describing Bernard: he is 'an outsider; [...] alien and alone'.[17] In a world centred on genetic modification and sameness, Bernard's physical defect is enough to isolate him from society, yet this isolation encourages Bernard to develop himself as an individual. He expresses to Lenina his desire to escape the constrictions of their society; he wants to feel 'More on [his] own, not

15 Ibid.
16 Ibid.
17 Aldous Huxley, *Brave new world* (London: Vintage, 2007), 56.
18 Ibid., 78.

19 Ibid., 136.
20 Gorman Beauchamp, 'The Shakespearean strategy of *Brave new world*', *Utopian Studies* 4 (1991): 61.
21 Ibid.

so completely a part of something else. Not just a cell in the social body', illustrating a need for individual thought in a repressive environment.[18] However, Bernard's questioning of societal norms is not a defiant act of personal integrity against this totalitarian state, but in reality is simply an expression of his longing to be accepted by society. When Bernard returns to civilisation with the savage, he is seemingly accepted by Alpha society:

> Success [...] completely reconciled him [...] to a world which, up till then, he had found very unsatisfactory. In so far as it recognized him as important, the order of things was good.[19]

Although Bernard still feels his individual self to be important, which defies the communal values of Fordian society, this order was only 'unsatisfactory' when it did not fully accept him. Bernard is content to be part of this society, and so fails to maintain his personal integrity. In contrast, John is completely opposed to this dystopian state, and fights for individuality and freedom. Beauchamp discusses the function of John in the text, noting that Huxley 'places the burden of challenging the brave new world on the individual shoulders of John Savage'.[20] John's mentality which allows him to condemn 'civilisation' stems from his childhood in the reserves, where 'crucial human values persist: concepts of personal worth and honor'.[21] Also key to John's ability to critique Fordian society, according to Beauchamp, is the influence of Shakespeare, which ensures that 'John emerges as, almost literally, a Renaissance man'.[22] John draws on Shakespeare to evaluate both society and himself; from evoking *Romeo and Juliet* to capture his feelings for Lenina, to interpreting Miranda's discourse in *The Tempest* as a message promoting societal change:

> 'Oh brave new world!' Miranda was proclaiming the possibility [...] of transforming even the nightmare into something fine and noble. 'O brave new world!' It was a challenge, a command.[23]

John takes it upon himself to try and free people from the constrictions of this society, but fails to rouse a sense of injustice in a group whose conditioning has influenced them to reject all conception of independence. Mustapha Mond tries to explain to John that there is an element of freedom within this civilisation in the form of the Alphas, who are 'separate and unrelated individuals' that are 'conditioned so as to be capable (within limits) of making free choice and assuming responsibilities'.[24] Yet at the beginning of the novel, Huxley reminds us that 'even Alphas have been well conditioned'; when Mustafa Mond mentions 'limits', he is essentially referring to anything that is considered unacceptable in the eyes of this totalitarian state, which demonstrates the lack of free will within this oppressive environment.[25] Thus, both *Brave new world* and *Romeo and Juliet* explore the Hegelian concept of tragic conflict between the individual and the state,

22 Ibid.
23 Huxley, 184–5.
24 Ibid., 195.
25 Ibid., 21.
26 Shakespeare, 1679.
27 Ibid.

and show the protagonists' upholding of personal integrity in the face of oppression. Although the patriarchy which governs *Romeo and Juliet* does not abolish the concept of individuality as a whole, it still dictates the actions of characters throughout the play. In contrast, given the added dimension of a dystopian setting, *Brave new world* acknowledges the desire for free will as defiance against a totalitarian society.

Synder's assertion that the tragic world is governed by inevitability is also apparent in both texts. The protagonists are doomed to fail given the context of oppression; just as *Romeo and Juliet* cannot truly escape the patriarchal system that governs them, the individualistic John cannot escape the conformist civilisation he has been brought into. These characters also suffer tragic consequences as a result of their stubborn persistence in maintaining their personal integrity, even when the system has punished them. Allusions to fate and destiny are apparent throughout *Romeo and Juliet*, most notably right at the beginning of the text in the prologue, which underlines that the entire plot is predeterined. The chorus reiterate the inevitability of the lovers' deaths throughout the prologue: 'their death-marked love' is ultimately 'fatal'; 'a pair of starcrossed lovers take their life.'[26] Significantly, the prologue makes note of the 'ancient grudge' between the two families before mentioning the fate of *Romeo and Juliet*, suggesting the impact this family feud has on their destiny.[27] The lovers fore-shadow their own misfortune in the play. Before he has even met Juliet, Romeo declares: 'I fear, too early: for my mind misgives /

Some consequence yet hanging in the stars', and even mentions 'untimely death'.[28] Again, Shakespeare evokes the image of the stars to suggest a sense of fate and inevitability: their destinies are written in the stars, and therefore cannot be altered. Juliet foreshadows Romeo's death as he descends from her balcony: 'I have an ill-divining soul! / Methinks I see thee, now thou art below, / As one dead in the bottom of a tomb', evoking the image of the tomb where both lovers perish.[29] Carroll recognises that 'in *Romeo and Juliet*, Shakespeare goes to great lengths to stress the inevitability of Capulet's vision',[30] namely that 'we were born to die',[31] another reference to the inescapability of death. However, without the existence of the patriarchal order which fuels the family feud and controls marriage, these lovers would not have had to rebel, and subsequently would not have died. Their untimely deaths are inevitable as a result of the family feud that prevents them from being together in a conventional way, which would otherwise satisfy both the needs to the patriarchy and the desires of *Romeo and Juliet*. Thus, the inevitability of this tragedy is rooted in the oppressive nature of the patriarchy, and *Romeo and Juliet*'s unwillingness to concede their love to appease this social structure.

Inevitability in *Brave new world* manifests itself in two ways: firstly, in the inescapable nature of this totalitarian society, predominantly as a result of conditioning, and secondly, through

28 Ibid., 1691.
29 Ibid.
30 Carroll, 55.

31 Shakespeare, 1691.
32 Huxley, 24.
33 Ibid., 12.

34 Ibid., 81.
35 Ibid., 36.
36 Ibid., 196.

John's inevitable failure to alter people's perception of the individual. The citizens of this dystopian world are predestined for a certain life before they are even exist, and are conditioned in their sleep throughout their youth by 'suggestions from the State.'[32] Commenting on this, the Director states: 'All conditioning aims at that: making people like their unescapable social destiny.'[33] In essence, people's minds are altered to influence their feelings and beliefs, meaning their social destiny is inevitable. An example of one of the phrases the public are conditioned with is: 'when the individual feels, the community reels', illustrating how this society has enslaved the minds of its people so that they are not only disgusted by individuality, but do not completely comprehend it as a concept given the emphasis on community the society promotes.[34] Mustafa Mond further highlights the inevitability of the continuing existence of this society. In chapter three, he likens society to a machine, commenting that: 'the machine turns, turns and must keep on turning—for ever'; the hyphen places emphasis on the phrase 'for ever', heightening this sense of inevitability.[35] Later in the text, he recounts the life of an average citizen in this society: 'his conditioning has laid down rails along which he's got to run. He can't help himself; he's fore-doomed', which again suggests the inevitability of the continuance of this social structure.[36] Despite the Controller's own individualistic character and passion for high art, he ranks social stability above these, favouring a functioning yet restricted society over the freedom of the individual. Thus, the suppression of individuality within this society is inevitable, as individuality is seen as a threat to stability, which is the most sacred value of this world. Consequently, John's resolve to free this society from the shackles of oppression is inevitably doomed to fail, as the citizens have been conditioned to see themselves as components of society rather than as individual entities. John even sees the members of society in this way: 'an interminable stream of identical [...] twins was pouring into the room. [...] Twin after twin, they came—a nightmare. Their faces, their repeated face', 'repeated indefinitely'.[37] This description notes the effect of cloning on identity through the repetition of the possessive pronoun 'their': they are simply one collective mass of identical twins that make up a larger body. After John fails to free the masses, he endeavours 'to escape further contamination by the filth of civilised life'.[38] However, John's attempts to isolate himself from society also fail. His self-flagellation is commercialised by civilisation, and people gather to watch him as if this is a comedic spectacle. Significantly, John concedes to the civilised people: 'acting on the word's suggestion he seized the bunch of knotted cords', suggesting that he is inherently trapped by this society, thus demonstrating the inevitability of his downfall.[39] John sacrifices his personal integrity by allowing civilisation to taint what was a sacred ritual; what was an independent act of repentance is converted into a meaningless orgy. John's efforts to maintain his individuality in a world of clones ultimately fails. Thus, inevitability is fundamental to both *Brave new world* and *Romeo and Juliet*, with particular emphasis on

37 Ibid., 183.
38 Ibid., 218.
39 Ibid., 225.
40 Synder, 391.

the protagonists' inability to escape the constraints of their respective repressive societies.

Thus, this essay can draw two conclusions: firstly, that dystopia is rooted in tragedy. Given their shared generic traits, most notably the conflict between the individual and the state, dystopian and tragic texts can be compared in terms of theories of tragedy. In addition to this, we can link Hegelian theories of tragedy with Synder's assertion that 'the tragic world is governed by inevitability, and its highest value is personal integrity', as both assert the importance of the individual.[40] Secondly, when relating these theories of tragedy to *Brave new world* and *Romeo and Juliet*, it becomes apparent that the tragic inevitability in the two texts is a result of the protagonists' persistence in maintaining their personal integrity despite opposition they face from the oppressive societal structures that dominate their respective tragic worlds. Whether this is a patriarchal system that prevents two lovers from being able to pursue a relationship whilst continuing to function as part of society, or a totalitarian state which eradicates all elements of individuality from a society dominated by the need for stability, the protagonists ultimately fail to overcome their oppressors. Significantly, a ll three protagonists commit suicide at the end of the texts: they cannot function independent of society with individual desires, as they cannot overcome the order society imposes on them. They pay the ultimate price for their inability to maintain personal integrity and overcome societal oppression.

Eleanor Slater

1   Emily-Rose Baker, 'The law of the fucking jungle', p. 209.
2   Aaron Saint John, 'Accountability', p. 148.
3   Chad Bentley, 'Census', p. 183.
4   Rebecca Sandeman, 'Boxes', p. 164.
5   Peter S Dorey, 'Cityscript', p. 26.
6   Grace Cohen, '3,943', p. 13.
7   Emily-Rose Baker, 'The law of the fucking jungle', p. 206.
8   Joe Caldwell, 'The best part of the afternoon', p. 12.

9   Peter S Dorey, 'Holes in the road', p. 200.
10   Ben Allen, 'Foxgloves', p. 4.
11   Mara-Daria Cojocaru, 'Nighthoney', p. 17.

Route 57, Issue Thirteen, 'The book is a collective too'

General Editor	Matthew Cheeseman
Editors	Emily-Rose Baker
	Amy Kinsman
	Mio Kobayashi
	Kristina Wearing

Design	Go! Grafik, www.gografik.ch
Paper	Munken Print White 1.5
Typeface	Rosart (Camelot), Buster
Printing	Graphius / New Goff, Ghent
Edition	600 copies

The editors gratefully acknowledge everyone who
bought a copy of Issue 12 and everyone who sold one:
thank you! We would especially like to thank the
Jessop West Café who stock our book all year round.

We also acknowledge the support of the University
of Sheffield's Faculty of Arts and Humanities Arts
Enterprise fund, the Centre for Poetry and Poetics,
the School of English and Amber's dad.

Finally, we thank everyone who submitted work for
Issue 13, or thought about it.

No profit shall be generated by dismantling these ruins.

Spirit Duplicator

SD8

ISBN: 978-0-907426-47-9

Spirit Duplicator is a small press founded in 2015 and named after the copier which prints a purple ink that supposedly causes intoxication when inhaled. We have our own spirit duplicator (a Roneo Model 50) but most of our pamphlets and books are printed using digital or risograph. We're interested in the interface between design and writing and are always looking to collaborate. Get in touch: www.spiritduplicator.org.

600 COPIES
PRINTED BY
GRAPHIUS